Praise for
THE SPIRITUAL GARDENER

*Winner of The New York City Big Book Award
in the category of home and garden.*

"When you open this book, you will be amazed at the wisdom of author Andrew Becker, who combines profound knowledge of gardening with a deep love of Jewish wisdom and spirituality. The quotations that he shares from the Torah, the Midrash, and the Chasidic Masters blend in seamlessly with the pragmatic suggestions on how to improve your horticultural skills. The Torah begins with Adam and Eve in the perfect Garden; with the help of this book you will find yourself transported to that primordial setting, or at least closer to it. Digging in the earth is holy work. Enjoy this wonderful book and give as a gift to like-minded friends and family members. Highly recommended."

Rabbi J.L. Mirel
Author of *Stepping Stones to Jewish Spiritual Living*

"Becker's prose reads without resistance, plying between the natural present and centuries of wisdom with insightful ease. His words slip into the reader's soul as deftly as pumpkin or squash seeds, or are nested in sentient soil like carrot grains on fertile seed tape. Here flower these meditations nurtured from Jewish roots and insightful horticultural dexterity. The book is divided into sections as natural and rhythmic as planting; its fruit bursts forth, cultivated, verdant, and ripe. As words are seeds themselves, this book offers from its leaves a bounty of horticultural wisdom, practical tips, spiritual inspiration, and a bounteous harvest."

Dr. Loss Pequeño Glazier
Digital Poetics (Alabama University Press) and *Anatman, Pumpkin Seed, Algorithm* (Salt)

"This is the perfect read for anyone who continues to wonder why he or she sticks fingers in the dirt and prays that a seed will grow. This inspirational miracle of horticultural prose is accompanied by evocative water color illustrations and meaningful religious quotations. I will gift this book to others who continue to ask me why I do what I do. It puts words to every gardener's life and experience since Adam graced Eden."

Kirk R. Brown
Converrsationist on Gardening Art, History and Business;
Leader of Programming as John Bartram and Frederick Law Olmsted;
Award-Winning Designer, Speaker, and Dramatist

With wry humor, earthy spirituality, and practical advice, lawyer and amateur gardener Becker tells the story of his own garden and entreats readers to plant, tend, harvest, and share their own soil in this fine debut. Explaining that he tries to live his life by the commandment of *bal tashchit* ("do not waste or destroy"), Becker explores different aspects of gardening and how they relate to his own spiritual thinking. He doles out tales of tending his garden, making peace with moles, slugs, and his neighbors who feed the rabbits he is determined to eject from their burrow under his garden. In an age when one can feel tethered to a phone and bombarded by information and news, Becker argues that tending to a garden allows for "sanctified time."

For Becker, troweling, watering, mulching, and seeding provide time to relish life, and also present opportunities for him to muse about the value of humility, how to divide chores in a marriage, and the ethics of hunting, among other topics. In uncomplicated, clear prose, Becker pleasantly urges readers—even those with just a balcony—to make a space where their home can be "infused with the Divine Presence." Green-thumbed spiritual readers will relish Becker's welcoming memoir.

(***BookLife***)

Praise for
THE SPIRITUAL FOREST

"Andy Becker has created another inspiring book that brings us closer to nature and to the spiritual side of life. Trees are the source of our physical sustenance but also serve as the quintessential Jewish metaphor for Torah in all its aspects. Read this book a bit at a time and you will be elevated to new levels of holiness."

Rabbi J.L. Mirel
Author of *Stepping Stones to Jewish Spiritual Living*

"This compact and wonderfully illustrated book brings readers a fresh perspective on why humans value and protect the arboreal world through the lens of rigorous religious scholarship and references, but with a light touch, evoking a nod of familiarity and conviction on every page. As a forest scientist who seeks ways to heighten the appreciation and conservation of trees, I will share this book near and far—to people of all experiences and faiths."

Nalini M. Nadkarni
Professor, School of Biological Sciences, University of Utah

"Andy Becker has done it again! This author has a habit of writing books that are spiritual, informative, and absolutely amazing. This time, it's *The Spiritual Forest*, and just as I was thinking, 'That's enough spiritual reading for the day,' Becker comes out with the astonishing idea that Adam may have been the first forest ranger. That's what he says!! This slender volume is not just a joyous hymn to the precious gift that trees are to the planet, but to myself—I have a picture in my mind of Adam in the Garden of Eden wearing his Smoky Bear hat and nothing else. You've got to read this book!"

Dorothy Wilhelm
Columnist, Broadcaster, Bestselling Author

"Andy Becker and I were high school friends and celebrated the first ever Earth Day together! He clearly still loves the earth and captures writing about why we need to take care of the earth from his Jewish tradition. Andy says, 'The actions we take to cultivate and guard trees are a service, not just to nature, but to humanity and creation.' I love how he writes from that remarkable notion and loved reading this book. Really nicely done and fun to read!"

Geoffrey L. Haskett
President, National Wildlife Refuge Association
Former US Fish and Wildlife Service Alaska Regional Director
Former US Polar Bear Commissioner
Former US Chief of the National Wildlife Refuge System

"*The Spiritual Forest* is many things: a spiritual guide, thoughtful prose, enlightening, encouragement, a call to arms (or shovels), but one thing it should never be is read quickly. This journey of reflection should be savored, like a feast that has been grown in one's private garden, harvested by hand, and prepared for friends. Throughout the well-crafted pages, it offers the reader an opportunity to ponder, provides resources for action, and most importantly, presents the need to look at our involvement and relationship with mother earth, the tree of life, from a different vantage point. Beautiful in its simplicity, each chapter melds the wisdom of the sages throughout time to one sole purpose, man's responsibility to protect nature and to teach the next generations to do the same. Exceptional and inspiring!"

"Just as others planted for me, I plant for future generations." – Talmud

Denise Frisino
Author/Speaker

"*The Spiritual Forest* is an inspiring and beautifully written work celebrating the preciousness of the earth and its glories. The vision is supported by a wide array of deep sources, drawn from both Jewish and non-Jewish traditions, along with practical suggestions for how to meaningfully contribute to the wellness and sustainability of our sacred home."

Rabbi Miles Krassen
PlanetaryJudaism.org

"Andy Becker makes a compelling spiritual case for environmentalism, without being preachy. Drawing from biblical passages, prophets, and sages, he shows rather than tells how the fate of our natural resources depends as much on our morality as our ingenuity. *The Spiritual Forest* inspires us to become long-term partners with nature."

Chris Bowman
Environmental Journalist

"It is a truly enriching experience to read Andy Becker's recent book, *The Spiritual Forest*. It provides a biblical basis for our responsibility to care for, nurture, and sustain our beautiful planet."

Graeme P. Berlyn, Ph.D.
E. H. Harriman Professor of Anatomy & Ecophysiology of Trees,
Yale School of the Environment

"As a man who has covered eight bare acres with a wide variety of trees over fifty years, and prefers to spend his Sunday mornings walking among them in my home-grown church, Andy Becker's *The Spiritual Forest* is the perfect biblical companion.

"It is a book to be read and absorbed slowly, perhaps sitting under a different leafy tree with each visit, contemplating the thoughts of Adam, the original park ranger, or Abraham, optimistically planting a tree in the desert.

"Each chapter brings more insight; personal change starts from within; our needed sustainability in a polluted world; the many blessings of fruit trees; the need to hold ourselves accountable in all situations; the utter joy in planting a tree and being able to sit quietly in its shadow in peace and happiness."

Bob Hill
Retired Book Author, Columnist, and Feature Writer
with the *Louisville Courier-Journal*

"Few authors can weave spirituality, conservationism, and principled, value-based living together as masterfully as Andrew Becker in *The Spiritual Forest*. Becker writes in clear and colloquial language that allows his philosophies, which are primarily based on Judaism, to permeate the hearts and minds of the staunchest pragmatists and devoted congregations at the same time. *The Spiritual Forest* is yet another book in the *Spiritual Gardener* series that resonates with a wide breadth of audiences and begs readers to slow down, notice the physical world around them, and consider deepening their relationship to the earth."

Christina Vega
Author of *Still Clutching Maps* and Publisher at Blue Cactus Press

"If you have ever wondered why God would create millions of unique and wondrous species—and then encourage us to wipe them out—Andrew Becker's *The Spiritual Forest* may enlighten you. According to Andrew, that was never God's plan at all, just our misguided interpretation of the commandment, 'Go forth and conquer the world!' Using our relationship with trees as a metaphor for how we interact with all of nature, Andrew Becker suggests that we *can* achieve a sustainable relationship with Mother Nature if we only extend the same reverence we reserve for spirituality to the natural world that supports us. Good advice indeed!"

Douglas Tallamy, Ph.D.
TA Baker Professor of Agriculture & Natural Resources
Department of Entomology and Wildlife Ecology
University of Delaware

THE SPIRITUAL GARDENER

Insights from the Jewish Tradition
to Help your Garden Grow

SECOND EDITION

ANDY BECKER

with illustrations by
ABIGAIL DRAPKIN

The Spiritual Gardener

Insights from the Jewish Tradition to Help your Garden Grow
Second Edition
The Spiritual Garden Series

Andy Becker

Published by Tree of the Field Publishing
www.AndyBecker.Life

TREE OF THE FIELD
——— PUBLISHING ———

ISBN: 978-1-7336698-9-4

Copyright © 2022 by Andy Becker. All rights reserved. No part of this publication may be reproduced, distributed, or transmitted in any form or by any means, including photocopying, recording, or other electronic or mechanical methods, without the prior written permission of the publisher, except in the case of brief quotations embodied in critical reviews and certain other noncommercial uses permitted by copyright law. For further information, please contact the author at andybecker.life@gmail.com.

Other Books by Andy Becker

The Spiritual Forest
Timeless Jewish Wisdom for a Healthier Planet and a Richer Spiritual Life

The Kissing Rabbi
Lust, Betrayal, and a Community Turned Inside Out

Cracking An Egg
Childhood Stories

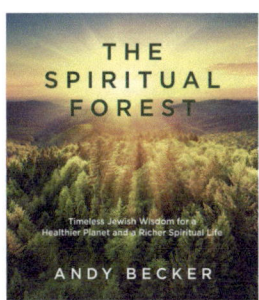
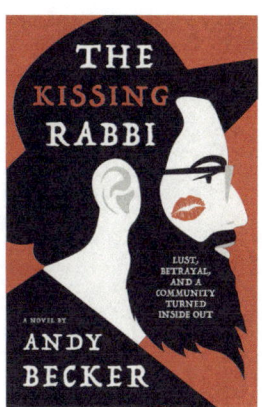

See Andy Becker's website and sign up for his newsletter at: andybecker.life

To my great loves and inspirations —
Donna, Matt, and Sam

Gan Eden

(Taking Action)

Now the Lord God took man, and He placed him in the Garden of Eden to work it and preserve it. ~ GENESIS 2:15

THE GARDEN of Eden may be long gone, but can we turn a finite stretch of dirt into something wondrous? If the Master of the Universe turned nothingness into perfection, can we feeble imitators transform an unused plot of ground into a beautiful and productive garden?

We are overstimulated, pulled in all directions, unable to digest all the news and information that bombards us. We fight traffic, repetitively read and update our smart devices, and rush here and there with quickened breath. Even if we possess all the material necessities of life, we may still suffer a longing. We lack something important: we are missing tranquility. Peace is nowhere to be found.

We can find tranquility in the garden. What happens when

we come home from a hard day's labor and we take a moment to water the vegetables? We observe nature at work and experience the joy of assisting it. We nurture and honor the miracle of creation. We revisit the completeness we felt when the vegetable bed was weeded and planted. We experience the beneficence of the garden even before we harvest it.

If humanity succumbed to its current predicament, after being born into a perfect world, what's to stop us from traveling in the opposite direction, heavenward, while here on earth? We can commence the redemption of humanity by noticing and caring for what is right around us.

With a connection to the garden we remind ourselves that we are part of the natural world. With simple tools, a shovel and a rake, we help orchestrate a special kind of music in a little plot of earth. We commune with the natural world as we feel our muscles and smell the dirt.

Like a Creator, we decide what to grow; for instance, broccoli. Our thoughts of weeding, planting, and watering the broccoli turn into action. We visualize the broccoli and we get to work. We are the thinkers and the doers; the broccoli does not think about growing. All the vegetables that we plant follow their natural course without intention or cogitation. By contrast, we choose how to spend our time. Why shouldn't we create a beautiful garden?

Where is your spot of earth? Every piece of land is as unique as the gardener who picks and cultivates it. Your garden will be like no other. Your garden will generate warmth, wonderment, and appreciation.

The first step may be the simple determination to move forward. Add a trowel and a hand tool to help with weeding, and you are in business. After that, pick a sunny spot, the sunnier the better. Watch how the sun shines across the garden. Try to run your rows north and south for fullest exposure. A flat spot is better than a sloping spot. If you are stuck with a slope, plant across to catch the rain and keep the soil from washing away. Mulch will also help the soil. It is going to get hot in the summer, so make sure you are near a faucet with a hose that reaches where it needs to go. Plant what you like to eat. Peas, lettuce, spinach, carrots, tomatoes, cucumbers, onions, and beets are easy to grow. Keep the taller plants in the back and the shorter plants upfront.

You are participating in a tradition as old as humankind. You have taken a divine step in the cycles of creation and nurturance. The food you grow will invariably lead you to thanksgiving and engagement with the world. You are inviting the Master of the Universe to His garden.

Seed Catalogs
(Do Not Waste)

When you besiege a city for many days to wage war against it to capture it, you shall not destroy its trees by wielding an ax against them, for you may eat from them, but you shall not cut them down.

~ Deuteronomy 20:19

One way to tilt the pinball machine of any marriage is to frequently complain about your spouse — to your spouse. A much healthier strategy is self-censorship. At least once a day I recommend employing the Spanish imperative, *"Cierra la boca!"* ("Hush your mouth!" in English). This adage especially applies to annoying things for which your spouse is only indirectly responsible. Catalogs, for example.

Over a course of years, an ever increasing influx of catalogs flooded our mailbox and ended up all over the house. I found them on the kitchen counter, next to the sofa in the family room, on the bedstands, and within arm's reach of the bathroom toilets. The inundation of catalogs started as a pre-Christmas phenomenon but morphed into a constant year-round barrage of slick, slippery little magazines with page after page of pictures of stuff and more stuff. As my lovely wife occasionally discovered, each time she bought a new thing from a catalog or merely shopped on the internet, the quantity of catalogs multiplied like fleas in a carpet on a hot day. She often expressed joy upon the arrival of her favorite catalogs, which I found grating.

I identified myself as a gardener, a man of the earth. I was philosophically opposed to the production and mailing of millions of pages of unwanted catalogs. The catalogs were anathema to me.

I also intuitively subscribed to the commandment of *bal tashchit* — do not waste or destroy. The commandment derives from Deuteronomy 20:19, proscribing the cutting down of trees during wartime. The learned sages and rabbis determined that if the Jews were prohibited from cutting down trees during extreme times of war, then it was even more sinful to kill trees or waste other valuable resources during times of peace.

Thus, the prohibition against waste was clear, and catalogs were a clear example of environmental destruction. In our mailbox we also often found repetitive solicitations for credit cards, houses for sale in the neighborhood, grocery store coupons, cars, financial planning, and politicians running for the latest election. If this wasn't waste, what was? As far as I was concerned, the violations of *bal tashchit* multiplied daily with the mail.

But people who live in glass houses shouldn't throw rocks. I soon realized that my own love of gardening involved unintended waste.

My sister, cognizant of my gardening activities, bought me a gift certificate for seeds from a company called Shepherd's Garden Seeds. Their catalog provided excellent descriptions of what would work for a garden in the short growing season of the Pacific Northwest. Shepherd's had many seeds that produced vegetables smaller than what is grown elsewhere but matured quicker, allowing for a successful harvest. I loved their peas, skinny bush string beans, lettuces, spinach, onions, and radishes, among many other seed packets. I spent time each winter reading their catalog and filling out my order. My receipt of the Shepherd's catalog was a happy moment during the cold and wet winter. The colorful pictures of the vegetables and flowers contrasted with the monotonous dreary gray skies outside.

Eventually, Shepherd's Garden Seeds was bought out by another company. My determined sister picked out a gift certificate from a different seed company that introduced me to something new: seed tape.

Seed tape is a wonderful invention. The seeds for carrots, lettuce, and onions are very small and difficult to grasp, and are aggravating to plant one seed at a time. Trying to space the tiny seeds in the dirt by shaking the packet spills out too many seeds. Seeds that sprout bunched too close together are difficult to thin out to allow for a good harvest. Seed tape eliminates these problems and frustrations: the little seeds are perfectly spaced on a piece of flimsy biodegradable tissue that rolls out in a perfect line. The seeds are planted efficiently with the correct spacing. The seedlings poke up from the dirt uniformly so they are easy to distinguish from any neighboring weeds. No longer are you wasting perfectly good seeds because they are grouped too close together. No longer do you feel frustrated trying to thin out a clump of sprouts.

My new-found enthusiasm for seed tape led me to search online for seed tapes from several companies. I didn't find one company that had all of the varieties of seed tape that I wanted to try. So I bought seed tapes from different companies.

The next winter I received an unremitting onslaught of

catalogs, suffocating in quantity, from all sorts of seed and garden companies. I was just as buried in gardening and seed catalogs as any of the catalogs my wife received. I saw myself as I was, just as much a wasteful consumer as a gardener. I had foolishly complained about catalogs to my wife. I unwittingly polluted the planet just as much as anyone else. With my philosophical leanings undercut, I now saw myself as a mildly detestable ecological hypocrite. My house turned to glass. My wife could now arm herself with a bucketful of rocks.

Rabbi Schneur Zalman of Liadi was once warned by his students that a certain individual was a hypocrite because he assumed pious customs and practices, holding himself out as a holy fellow when his mind and heart remained unrefined. The Rabbi referred his students to a section in the Talmud where it describes the ill-effects of hypocrisy. The Rabbi explained that one who makes of himself more than he is in matters of righteousness and piety will eventually find that these false traits have become engrained in his character.

We waste unbelievable amounts of resources. No one is immune, including well intentioned gardeners like you and me. As home gardeners, however, we also make a modest stand for a healthier and more balanced world. We break the chain of transportation, processing, food sales, chemical fertilization, and refrigerated storage. We lessen our individual environmental footprint. If we can do that as home gardeners, we can raise our own consciousness about breaking the cycle of waste. We can promote good nutrition, health and balance within our own families. We can obey the commandment of *bal tashchit* and still read our seed catalogs. But if you start to feel smug, beset by thoughts of superior moral convictions, you can simply say to yourself, *"Cierra la boca!"*

Turn Over
(Transformation)

Soil is the stage from which all things — good, beautiful, vicious, creative, dull, outrageous and evil — emerge. A teaspoon of living earth contains five million bacteria, twenty million fungi, one million protozoa, and two thousand algae. Amoebas slide over sand grains hunting bacteria. Bacteria swim through micro worms like soil hyenas, devouring almost anything. There are about 9,500 kinds of soil in the United States and no one has ever tried to create sanctuaries for any of them. ~ Peter Warshall, The Whole Earth Catalogue

Wherever people stand is holy ground. Whatever spot on earth you occupy can be sanctified to God.
~ Elimelech of Lyzhansk (Hasidic Master)

THERE are many kinds of turnovers: a basketball player dribbles the ball off his foot out of bounds, giving possession of the ball to the other team. A turnover is a sweet pastry with some fresh apple inside. Relatives are said to turn over in their graves when there's unpleasant gossip about a family member going about. As we age, we turn over in bed to trade one arthritic ache for another.

In the garden, I turn over the soil.

While it may seem like it is still winter in the month of March, tulips pop up and the cherry blossoms greet the cold and wet. The raised garden beds beckon, despite the chill and dampness. Ignoring creaky knees and a worn-out spine, shrugging off an occasional sprinkle from the sky, I find the old pointed shovel. Locating the hand trowels may require several trips through the greenhouse, shed, and garage. The frustration of searching for tools put away last fall is a yearly ritual. They didn't disappear; I'll find them.

I turn over the dirt with a shovel, and then I get on my knees and break up the dirt, pulling out the weeds with a hand tool. My favorite tool for this is called a cobra head. It has a little spade on the end of a boomerang curve of metal that lets me weed or plow the dirt that I turned over with the shovel by hand. The other hand tool I like, a hand cultivator, has three diagonally pointed spikes that I plunge into the soil and then twist with my wrist. Armed with my pointed shovel, cobra head, and pointed spike cultivator, the only question is how many beds I can get done before various bodily pains tell me to call it a day.

If you have neck and back issues, I recommend the table top position where you use your dominant hand for tilling and the other hand and knees for support. Or you might change positions frequently from table top to sitting on one's knees or derrière. You should expect pain and stiffness later that day. A healthy supply of Ibuprofen and a roll-on topical analgesic like Biofreeze may lessen the pain. A cold pack or frozen bag of peas may also help.

When I hand till, I like to use an old piece of thick cardboard on the ground to lessen the accumulating wetness and mud on my knees. Soggy pants tend to sag and become uncomfortable. Slide a piece of cardboard around the raised bed and use the hand tools to nicely break up the dirt clods that the shovel turned over. You may find some roots of last year's plants or weeds, including some very fine white strands. These will form weeds of the future and may be easily removed to preclude just that.

While you may want to rush to avoid the monotony of this kind of work, my advice is to slow down. The better the preparation of the soil, the better the garden. Meticulous preparation pays big dividends.

You will undoubtedly uncover some earthworms. Treat each worm reverently. As the great Charles Darwin opined, "It may be doubted whether there are many other animals which have played so important a part in the history of the world, as have these lowly organized creatures." The earthworm is your friend, aerating and mixing the minerals of the soil with the organic matter, improving the richness and fertility of the dirt. You need not add any chemical fertilizers to sweeten the soil of the garden bed; in fact, to do so may injure your amigos, the earthworms, who enjoy slightly acidic soil. Turn over the soil, remove the old roots and weeds, cultivate by hand, and add a little compost and peat moss. Refrain from compressing the soil by walking on it. You'll end up with very good dirt, and the earthworms will enjoy a fine home.

Once you circumnavigate the first vegetable bed with hand tools, methodically discarding any weeds, and breaking up all the dirt, the dirt needs to be leveled out with a rake. Radishes, spinach, kale, onions, lettuce, carrots, broccoli, and peas are the first seeds to go in the dirt. I recommend seed tape for the onions, lettuce and carrots. The size of the seed dictates how deep to plant. Seeds for radishes and spinach are big enough to plant individually without any spacing problems. In a raised bed with carefully tended soil, seeds can grow a little closer together.

The work of turning over the soil and planting early spring seeds is a humbling act of faith and joy. You are participating in the creation, wonder, and miracle of life. What grows will be superior in taste, color, and freshness to anything for sale in the store. In just a few months, friends and neighbors may marvel at your hard work and green thumb. They may "ooh" and "aah" at what you accomplished. Even your family is impressed; however, you are unlikely to brag about your garden because you know that the worms deserve more credit.

And what of the seeds themselves? I decide where and when to plant the seeds, their depth, and how much to water them. But I am only setting the table. The seed must first unite sufficiently with the dirt to decay and lose its old form and identity. Only then may it emerge as something new. The exact moments of these metamorphisms for all the seeds are close but not the same in time. Each seed passes through some sort of natural abyss that separates the old from the new.

Perhaps the most famous seed in modern history was nicknamed Methuselah, one of several date palm seeds preserved in an ancient jar discovered during excavations at Herod the Great's palace at Masada in Israel. Radiocarbon analysis confirmed that the seeds dated from 155 BC to 64 AD.

After the seeds were stored at a university in Tel Aviv for forty years, three of the seeds were planted and one sprouted. The sprout turned into a tree that has grown successfully to produce flowers and pollen. This is the only living representative of the Judean date palm, a tree that was extinct for over 1800 years.

Each of the vegetable seeds that you buy in packets are no less a miracle than the Methuselah seed. The potential that exists in each seed is its own little miracle.

Similarly, the yearly ritual of turning over the dirt and planting anew invokes the miracle of transformation and creation. Is the seed's transformation analogous to the spiritual forces sleeping within us? We bury the seed slightly below the ground. Can we likewise push down our selfish inclinations, ever so gently, to hasten the sprouting of our own true natures? As we turn over the dirt in the garden, can we begin refining our souls to reach our full potential?

Tick Tock, Early Spring Gardener

(Time Management)

Everything has an appointed season, and there is a time for every matter under the heavens: A time to plant and a time to uproot the planted.

~ Kohelet (Ecclesiastes) 3:1-2

Beets, radishes and spinach are easy to grow in colder or milder climes. Their seeds are among the first that can be directly planted into the garden bed in early spring. These seeds will survive colder temperatures and a little frost. Unlike other root vegetables with little tiny seeds, the beets, radishes and spinach are the champions of early spring, and their seeds are big enough to space easily. Carrot, onion, and leek seeds are planted at a lesser depth, and thus need to wait until things warm up. Not so with beets, radishes and spinach. The beet, radish and spinach seeds are screaming,

"Plant me! Plant me!" The eager gardener heeds the call, springing into action.

The tuned-in gardener benefits by seeding the first vegetables as soon as the season allows, to maximize the growing season. Thus, the garden teaches time management and the importance of seizing the moment. However, the garden also teaches patience, and the importance of waiting to plant the seeds that come later. If we are over-anxious and plant too soon, the seeds will not sprout. Timing is everything. As we gain more experience, we also want to space out seed plantings so we don't harvest everything all at once. To make the garden meaningful and beneficent, we recognize that what we plant and when we plant it determines what we will harvest tomorrow. The enthusiastic gardener wants to meld with the seasons and succumb to the predictable powers found in nature.

The seasons and the weather are manifestations of the passage of time and order in the universe. Outside the garden, we fight against the clock. We never have enough time. We rush here and there, worrying about being on time. We feel frustrated when we waste time. We know that we will ultimately run out of time — and back into the earth we'll go, to push up daisies. The clock is always ticking.

The spiritual gardener, however, does not think about

time antagonistically, instead counting on nature's seasonal stability to provide soil, light, water, and warmth for the garden to flourish. An awareness of time, even if subconscious, is a critical element of successful gardening.

The experienced gardener who springs into action when the beds are ready for the first early spring seedings feels botanically attuned. The seeds have a purpose that the gardener is trying to unleash and awaken. Your time in the garden may help you unleash and awaken your awareness of the precious moments of each day of your life.

As you breathe the air and smell the dirt, you exercise body and mind together. You are living meaningfully. Time becomes a friendly alarm clock instead of an annoying enemy.

A slave has no time of his or her own. Every minute of the slave's day belongs to the slave's master. A free person is someone exercising his or her own will to decide how to spend their time. As the great sages stated, the day is short and the tasks are many. When we choose to work in the garden we are not slaves to worldly, self-inflicted pressures. We are exactly where we are supposed to be. The garden allows us to sanctify time.

The seeds of the purple beet, red radish, and leafy green spinach germinate exactly when they are supposed to. Each seed is neither too early nor too late. As the great physicist

Erwin Schrodinger wrote in 1933, "It is a miracle that in spite of the baffling complexities of the world, certain regularities in nature can be discovered." You can discover those regularities in your garden. Being a gardener means living happily in the space and time afforded to you. You are both found and lost in your tasks. The time flies by as the seeds go in the ground.

One early spring day, the sun will burst through the afternoon clouds just as the gardener's tasks are completed. The gardener will not head inside, but stay put, to linger — and feel the sun's warmth, a harbinger of the coming days. This may be a time for the gardener to do nothing more than look at what has been sown so far, breathe the dirt and the air, and to listen to what the birds have to say. Some of the key moments in the garden occur when you pause and, without even thinking about it, internalize the tick tock of the seasons.

Creepy Crawly
(Metamorphosis)

Why were human beings created last in the order of Creation? So that they should not grow proud — for one can say to them, 'Even the gnat came before you in creation!'
~ Tosefta Sanhedrin 8:3

There are good bugs and bad bugs, bugs that fly around, and all sorts of things that creep and crawl in the garden. Often, I don't know if a bug is a good bug or a bad bug. I don't like to encounter creepy crawly things. However, over time I have gained curiosity and lost some of my aversion to the creepy world. I've decided to co-exist with bugs, so I avoid sprays, powders, and grains that are sold to kill bugs. Although I don't want creepy crawly things eating my vegetables, I also don't want any chemicals near the food that I eat, especially anything that is powerful enough to kill living things.

Even if a bug is not a particularly good bug, I can choose not to be bothered by it. An example is the crane fly. A crane fly looks like a giant mosquito, and I see them around the lawn during early fall. They come and go. They don't bite like mosquitos, or if they do, they don't bite me. The crane flies do not seem to hurt the lawn, the flowers in the flower beds, or what's left of the vegetables in the garden beds. So I can ignore bugs like the crane flies if I don't see them causing any damage.

I do not always shun chemicals and poisons. I use them on slugs, for example, for slugs will greatly damage the garden if allowed to proliferate. The slugs crawl here and there at night, sliming around until they find my flowers and vegetables. They attack my vegetables like hungry football players at an all-you-can-eat buffet. They are strangely particular at times, destroying just enough of each precious plant to render it unappetizing. Slugs are wonderfully beneficial when it comes to composting the bed of the forest. However, I am not growing a forest; I am growing a garden.

Whenever I find a slug I pick it up and plunk it into our big blue yard waste container. The lid on the yard waste container prohibits the slug's escape. The slugs that end up there are transported once a week with the yard waste to the local dump and ground into compost. The compost is used by the county and sold to the public. No one holds a memorial service for these unlucky creepers.

The problem with picking up a slug is its slime. The slime of a slug adheres like a sticky, snotty cement and does not easily wash off your fingers. So I grab some gloves or hand tools to scoop up the slug and plink it into the garden waste container. Although this may feel a little creepy at first, with years of practice, you can do it without any shivering or other symptoms of revulsion.

I have tried various home remedies, but leaving out bowls of beer is a waste of beer. Salting the yard likewise seems wasteful and is ultimately ineffective, given the frequent rain where I live. I recommend a pet-friendly slug bait, applied liberally and early in the springtime to the places where slugs have appeared in the past. I also endorse sprinkling the perimeters of the garden to avoid using slug bait where you grow food.

Other bugs that can cause as much damage as the infamous slugs are surely present when multiple holes appear in the leaves of the vegetable plants, most notably cabbages and Brussel sprouts. The leaves get infected by little wormy bugs with names like cabbage worm, root maggot, cutworm, or spittlebug. I don't spray the infected vegetables — I pull them up and throw them in the compost container. I cut my losses.

After several seasons of losing a specific crop, I may completely abandon attempts to grow that plant in that same space. I go with what is successful. My lettuces and broccoli seem to grow without any bug damage, while I have struggled with different kinds of cabbages.

One strategy that seems to work for cabbage is placing little thin discs around the stem or trunk of the plant where it meets the soil. The disc has a little slit so it snugs around the base of the vegetable. The disc discourages the wormy bugs from crawling out of the dirt and onto the cabbage. Another strategy is to grow the infected vegetable in a different spot. Maybe the offending bugs are not everywhere every year. Another option is to grow the vegetable in a pot on an old abandoned table so that it is elevated off the ground in the event the bugs are reaching the plant by ground rather than air. This doesn't mean that the offending bug cannot also climb up a table, but it is easy enough to lift up the pot to see what is hiding on its underside. Make sure to water the pots on the table more frequently than the plants in the beds during the hottest days of summer.

Some years I see a lot of pill bugs, little gray armadillos that roll into a protective ball when endangered. They come out at night and will mow down a row of seedlings if one isn't paying attention. Like slugs and many other bugs, they like the dark and the wet. They love to hang out during the day under an old piece of wood. The best way to deal with these bugs is to clean up around your garden beds.

Wriggly, skinny crawlers like centipedes give me a little shot of the creeps when I am weeding the vegetable bed. I don't see a lot of them so I leave them alone, especially if they are just in the dirt and not on the plant. Beetles may mildly freak me out when weeding. I might give the centipede or beetle a gentle fling out of the vegetable bed, but since I don't know which centipede or beetle is doing me a favor, I let nature take its course, usually opting to ignore the bug's presence in the vegetable bed.

One year I noticed a very colorful flying bug loitering on the raspberry leaves. Raspberry canes grow like weeds and have been wonderfully prolific; each year we make a lot of jam to give away. Making the jam has become an important yearly ritual for us. Thus, I was seriously alarmed when I saw little winged flying creatures on our precious line of berries where we grow them along the fence. I saw, however, that the bugs were not eating the fruit and did not seem to hurt the leaves. I guessed that the bugs were possibly eating some sort of smaller aphid-sized bugs on the raspberries and therefore possibly serving a useful function. Again, when it comes to bugs, the old adage that discretion is the better part of valor applies.

Trial and error has led me to grow plants that appear to coexist with the bugs in my area. I like to grow beets, onions, leeks, spinaches, lettuces, carrots, cucumbers, carrots, zucchini, spaghetti squash, and tomatoes. Likewise, I try to coexist with the bugs when weeding, even when they creep me out.

I do not suffer a hysterical meltdown like some folks who start to yell and jump around when they see a spider or a hornet. Likewise, a spider, colony of ants, or infrequent stinging insect in the garden doesn't set me off.

Still, many things that creep and crawl or fly around are repulsive. Whether a specific creature, like the worm, provides a wonderful benefit or, like the mosquito, appears to serve no discernible purpose other than sucking blood and spreading disease, all the creatures visible to the naked eye in the garden are alive. As such, they are constantly on the move and seeking the means to survive, just as we are. They are found in all environments where we live. Some are pollinators that are essential to many of the flowering vegetables that we wish to grow. As such, humans are dependent on things that creep and crawl and fly around. Without them, the earth would suffer great devastation and destruction.

Insects also undergo metamorphosis. They don't grow like

we do, or like the birds or the other mammals. Instead, they transform themselves in stages, sometimes turning into completely different creatures. The classic example is the caterpillar, who hatches from an egg and crawls around eating leaves until it eventually forms a chrysalis and then becomes a butterfly. The transformations that take place in the insect world are often mind-boggling.

After many years of gardening, my revulsion towards bugs has receded. I've developed an acceptance and respect for that which creeps or crawls or flies around. I marvel at the diversity of life in and near the soil, appreciating the perpetual interaction of animals that creep and crawl in nature.

I've also noticed that there are times when I am sufficiently immersed in my simple tasks to become a part of the ongoing, rhythmic metamorphosis of the garden itself. I feel the energy of the garden instead of the aches and pains in my body. Perhaps I've learned a kind of intimacy with the garden from the insects which appear to be one with their natural environs. Unlike an insect's dramatic physical changes, the spiritual gardener may undergo a metamorphosis in attitude, simply from observing the things that creep and crawl until feelings of aversion disappear. Perhaps a change in your reactions may derive from the simple practice of toiling in the garden. Is it possible to feel oneness with all of God's creatures, even those that creep and crawl?

Weeds
(Humility)

*Master of the universe grant me the ability to be alone;
May it be my custom to go outdoors each day among the trees and grass,
among all growing things; and, there may I be alone to enter into
prayer, there I may express all that is in my heart talking to you, the
one to whom I belong.* ~ Rabbi Nachman's Prayer:
Rabbi Nachman of Bratslav (18th–19th c.)

Tulips and daffodils burst forth with color after months of soggy cold and gray skies. While the buds on the rhododendrons plump up, the spiritual gardener has been out shoveling and turning, troweling and raking, planting the first seeds.

The radishes come up first, followed by the spinach and the lettuce in the raised beds. By the time the beet seeds pop up, the garden beds also show the first signs of weeds. Young weeds grow quickly, but are distinguishable from the seedlings

of the vegetables that were planted in a row. The weeds will appear no matter how thoroughly you prepared the soil. The sooner the little weeds are picked out the better. Intensive weeding at the end of the gardening season, adding compost and mulch, and covering the beds with a sheet of weed block, year by year, builds the soil, and cuts down the weeds.

Weeding the vegetable beds is an exercise that you should repeat every few weeks until the vegetables are harvested. Every once in a while I will hear someone say that they like weeding. These folks probably also like going to the dentist. Clean teeth are nice, but you don't want to hold your mouth open while someone inserts shiny metal instruments that poke and scrape in there, droning on with small talk.

Weeding isn't quite the same, but it's certainly uncomfortable to be crouched and bent over, reaching and pulling, and becoming stiff, sore, damp and dirty. In addition to the physically uncomfortable nature of weeding, there is also loneliness. I can think of many times our friends came over to eat our strawberries, beans and cucumbers, but I cannot think of a single instance when anyone came over to help weed. Weeding is usually a solitary pursuit, just like walking down the hallway to the dentist's chair. The discomfort, however, is finite. With determination, the weeds will be removed to the compost bin, and the vegetables can grow in their rows without unwanted competition. Looking at a freshly weeded bed feels as good as leaving the dentist's office, but without a bill. You also learn to enjoy the bugs and the birds for company. You tune out the noise of urban life.

The longer the weeds are ignored, like a cavity, the more the gardener will suffer. The horsetail weed is a prime example. This invasive plant has long and deep roots that love to spread horizontally underground. Horsetails are easy to break off at the surface, but that will not slow their propagation as they can grow back and cover the flower bed within weeks. The only thing to do is to dig down and follow the horsetail's root until you can grab as much of it as possible. If the dirt is soft enough, you may pull up several horsetail plants all connected to the same thicker underground root, like an umbilical cord tethered to sextuplets. By getting as much of the horsetails as possible, you will hopefully keep them to a minimum even if you cannot completely eliminate them. The horsetail weed has been around longer than your garden and you will likely perish before the horsetails in your garden go away. While this may sound gloomy, the point is to respect one's adversary. Laziness in March, April, and May will lead to gardening mayhem in June, July, and August. If you don't regularly attack the weeds, they will get ahead of you.

Another insidious weed that likes to choke ornamental plants to death is the morning glory, snaking up the plant with a vine like a curving silly string and hiding up the branches. It grows vigorously even under weed block, and needs only a crack of daylight to tangle around one's favorite rhododendron with uncanny speed. You need to pull it out and pull it out and pull it out, and most of all, never let it flower and spread more seeds. When it comes to weeding, don't dawdle — attack! The lessons to learn are toil and determination.

Weeding also involves humility. You bow down on your knees in the dirt, preoccupied with a task requiring no education, skills, or qualifications. You are not sitting on a lofty throne, giving orders, exploiting the fruits of another's labors. You surrender selfish and narcissistic impulses. In this sense, weeding can take on a prayer-like quality, as you humbly and quietly care for that which is in a continual state of creation. There is a value to working physically and quietly. You can hear your own thoughts merge into a meditative state. Your solitude is invigorated by the dirt, the worms, the air, and your physicality. The toil becomes an antidote to the stresses of the modern world.

To regularly weed the garden is to cultivate order, to beat

back an encroaching wild state, to purposefully nurture the food that you are growing. The plants are hardy and programed to grow themselves but they are also preciously fragile, and you are their steward. The plants are not your children, but you take responsibility for their growth. You feel rewarded in the present as you improve the health and aesthetics of the garden, and you will be rewarded in the future as you harvest the freshest and most delicious food that you ever tasted. You feel a fine sense of accomplishment as each bed is weeded.

A cleanly weeded vegetable or flower bed is pleasing to the eye and inflates the gardener's ego like a starlet's visit to the mirror before the Academy Awards. But there's more to the gardener's pride than that. A row of broccoli, like miniature trees, neatly lined up next to a row of dusky-colored crinkly Italian kale means that civilization has temporarily vanquished nature's unremitting conquering forces. The devil's friends, starvation and deprivation, will not beset you. The gardener who consistently pulls the weeds thus makes a statement.

The term "humility" comes from the Latin word *humilitas*, which may also be translated as "grounded" or "from the earth." Weeding literally grounds us, triggering a most humble prayer-like meditation. Humbled, we enjoy an intimate front row seat to the choreography of nature's never-ending dance. Our prayers are best uttered with humility, awe, and respect for the natural world.

Lawn Envy
(Valuing What Really Matters)

Envy, lust and honor-seeking drive a person from the world.
~ Pirkei Avoth 4:21

My girlfriend and I rented two houses in Tacoma before we got married, one in South Tacoma and the other in East Tacoma, each for over a year. Each little house was surrounded by lawn. I was responsible for mowing the lawn. During the time we lived in each rental, my lawn mower got stolen at each place, once out of a detached garage, and once out of a fenced yard. After the second theft, in a pique of antisocial resentment towards my neighborhood, I let the lawn grow until it was so high that I had to cut it with a weed whacker.

These lawns weren't that big and I was young, so mowing

wasn't really a chore. What was a chore was getting the lawnmower started. That's where my girlfriend came to the rescue. After I had yanked on the starter cord long and hard enough to pull my arm out of its socket, my girlfriend took a turn at it. Usually, with one or two determined pulls, at most three, the mower would catch and drown out my sounds of exhilaration that a miracle had occurred.

I studied her technique. She frowned and pushed her bottom lip up and over the upper as she spread her feet and bent her knees, and geared up for her big two-handed pull. My job was to put my foot on the mower's frame so it wouldn't move. Maybe her arm was just short enough to create the correct physics. My attempts to adjust the choke, the cord, the angle, check the sparkplug and gas, and whatever curses I thought of between each tug and yank, were all for naught. She had the magic touch.

About five years later, after we'd married and our second child was born, we moved to a neighborhood in a development with bigger houses and bigger lawns. We had a large, steeply sloped front lawn that was difficult to mow and served no purpose other than decoration. I pulled and pushed a brand new self-propelled lawnmower while walking horizontally across the hill; turning the mower was a miserable task due to the exaggerated slope. Even with the self-propelling feature I could not push the mower up the lawn, and mowing downhill would have risked a runaway.

Up the street on the corner sat a house on a giant flat lot with an enormous dark green lawn. Their lawn was perfect, without dandelions or dry spots, and wonderfully uniform, with richer looking grass than a major league baseball park. The owners, active senior citizens, spread some sort of rich dirt on it every spring. The man looked so very happy caring for the lawn. He was frequently edging, mowing, raking leaves or spreading his magic fertilizing dirt. One could tell he took enormous pride in his lawn.

I experienced both annoyance and envy at the man's happiness. I didn't have a dog at that time. If I had, I would have brought the dog by to take as many dumps on that lawn as possible. After a time, I shared my jealousy with my wife and young children, disparaging the corner house as owned by a couple of old show-offs who had nothing better to do than to cultivate a perfect lawn.

The man with the perfect lawn looked happiest when he was mowing the lawn on his riding mower. At the time, consumed by my covetousness, I grumbled that the man looked stupid, like an imitation farmer, growing a crop of vanity. I regularly disparaged the perfect lawn, the man's riding lawn mower, and the man when we drove by.

My critical view of the suburban riding mower would change by necessity. We moved to our third and present house where it took me too long to mow the lawn with the self-propelled walking mower. My next door neighbor took an interest in my labors and explained that I needed a riding mower. He knew where I should go, to the lawn and garden dealership for the John Deere tractors.

Off I went to buy a shiny new John Deere 42" deck riding mower in Tacoma accompanied by my wife, checkbook in hand, next door neighbor, and both children. My life soon changed. Mowing became a form of calming recreation, no longer a chore. I quickly mastered adjusting the deck height, engaging the mower, turning and reversing. As easy as driving a car, up and down the lawn I went, making enough noise to zone everything out, riding the John Deere like a real suburban lawn farmer.

The beauty of the riding mower is that one accomplishes an aesthetic feat without exertion, yet with enough noise pollution to trumpet one's masculinity. While I may mount the John Deere with a general malaise or specific frustrations, I dismount feeling much better after my mastery of nature proves that I am the chief, the Boss, the master mower of all time.

Over time, my family noticed my devotion to the mower. Accordingly, I soon owned various tchotchkes: a John Deere baseball cap, t-shirt, keychain, coffee cup, plastic street sign that said, "John Deere Avenue" and a paperweight of a little green John Deere mower. The John Deere was even given an affectionate family nickname; "Johnny". It was Johnny who facilitated not only a lawn that was pleasing to the eye, but a playing field for spirited badminton and croquet games over the course of many summers.

After several years of consistent, frequent mowing, one day in early springtime, the mowing deck fell off the mower, bringing the entire operation to a halt in mid-mow. One of the welds holding the little wheel to the mower deck sheared off, a product of too many tight turns at speed over bumpy ground. Suddenly, Johnny was down. Since it was mowing season, the John Deere dealer was backed up for ten weeks on repairs.

Consumed with feelings of sadness when Johnny was carted away for a long separation, I could hardly bid my mower a fond farewell without choking up. While he was away from home, my loneliness and sense of longing grew along with the grass. The feelings were palpable, akin to quitting smoking or watching one's child leave for college.

Lawn envy had once induced me to disparage a neighbor, yet conversely behave like a king years later when I had my own perfect lawn. These feelings derived, no doubt, from a competitive urge within, even though I didn't realize that I was competing and there was no victory to achieve. Without consciously thinking about it, I had succumbed to a cultural view of the front lawn as a symbol of the American middle-class dream. My mind was unconsciously polluted with the view that people who meticulously trimmed their lawns were not just the best of neighbors, but superior human beings who had their lives in order.

There is nothing intrinsically wrong with a nice lawn. I would not trade the fun family times playing badminton and croquet on that lawn for anything. While I understand the magic of Gertrude Stein's proverb "A rose is a rose is a rose," a nice lawn is just a nice lawn, and it pretty much stops there. There is no deeper level of resonance. What was absurd was how much emotional weight I attached to it.

I am envious by nature, imbued with desires and emotions, and in that tendency I am not alone. Inequality, and therefore envy, are intrinsic to the human condition. However, we would do better to envy those neighbors who are wiser, kinder, more generous, and more knowledgeable than we, regardless of the conditions of their lawns. If we envy the authentic good in someone else, we can motivate ourselves to improve our little bit of the human condition, without relying on a lawn tractor to create a false self-esteem. The same competitiveness that feeds envy can also lead to discerning and redirecting our own emotions.

All this is worth thinking about the next time I zone out while riding up and down the lawn, on good ol' Johnny.

Damn Wabbits

(Esau-type Feelings)

It should not be believed that all beings exist for the sake of the existence of man. On the contrary, all other beings too have been intended for their own sakes and not for the sake of anything else. There is no difference between the pain of humans and the pain of other living beings, since the love and tenderness of the mother for the young are not produced by reasoning, but by feeling.
~ Rabbi Moses Maimonides, Guide for the Perplexed

My first memory of a rabbit is Bugs Bunny. As kids we spent hours in front of the black and white T.V. watching Warner Brothers cartoons. Bugs was long and skinny and gray. I am not sure I liked his smart-aleck persona. The arrogance of Bugs Bunny rubbed me the wrong way.

My next memory of a rabbit is as fuzzy as rabbit fur. Maybe I saw some bunnies at a petting zoo or at a pet store. Those rabbits were puffy, snow white like a cotton ball. They did not seem real. They looked so soft. My brother and I each had our own rabbit's foot, but I think that they were synthetic; at least I never related them to an actual rabbit.

Half my life passed without thinking much about rabbits.

After we moved into our current residence, I developed strong feelings about rabbits. My gardening took off. After years of battling shade and poor soil, rocky terrain, and hills, I was finally living somewhere with great sun exposure, soil that drained well, and a flat yard. I could garden to my heart's content under favorable conditions. My passion for gardening exploded. Each year was better than the last.

After a few years of gardening bliss, my family and I started to notice rabbits in our neighborhood. We usually saw them at night, often frozen in their tracks by the car's headlights as I drove into our driveway. During the day they would likewise freeze when they saw us on foot and then scamper across the yard in fright, ducking under the fence. These rabbits were brown and mangy looking, but at first we delighted in seeing them, much like when we saw a deer on the side of the road. Spotting an occasional rabbit in the neighborhood or in our own yard was fun.

That was before the population explosion. After just one

summer, the neighborhood's rabbit population boomed. Something was chewing and destroying my spinach, carrot tops, onion tops, lettuce, and kale. It was, in the immortal words of the great Elmer Fudd, "the damn wabbits!" You name it, and the damn wabbits were out there eating it.

It was an epidemic. After all that weeding, shoveling, hand tilling, leveling and raking, seeding, more weeding, and watering, my labors were for naught. The damn wabbits came at night like starving, nose twitching, nervous bandits, seemingly intent on destroying the garden. In response, soon I became like a psychopathic Mr. McGregor with blood lust for every hop-a-long.

Instead of a happy jaunt from the house to inspect the garden after work, tragedy spoiled my view, as the heretofore beautiful line of miniature broccoli trees looked like irregularly massacred hedges. The rows of string beans were eaten down to the nubs. Adding to the frustration, the damn wabbits often took just a bite here and a bite there of each plant. This was possibly an instinct embedded in rabbit DNA, to make sure the plants would continue to produce more rabbit food. Each beautiful strawberry, for example, was missing a rabbit's mouthful. By taking just enough of a bite to ruin the plant for human consumption, I felt that the rabbits were taunting me.

I was never pro-guns. I was a teenager when James Earl Ray shot Martin Luther King, Jr. and Sirhan Sirhan shot Bobby Kennedy. Thus, without really studying the issue, I supported gun control long before the epidemic of mass shootings in America.

No one in my immediate or extended family owned guns or hunted. Interestingly, I learned years later that the only hunters in the Bible were Nimrod and Esau, two ignoble fellows of exceedingly ill repute. Nimrod helped his cohorts build the infamous Tower of Babel, and he also threw the world's first great proponent of monotheism, Abraham, into the fiery furnace. Esau not only sold his birthright to his younger twin brother Jacob for a bowl of red lentil stew, but he also threatened to kill his brother as soon as the period of mourning for their father Isaac was over. Thus, the only hunters mentioned in the Bible were rotten characters.

I was uninformed and had never even thought about the moral implications involved in hunting animals until confronted with the bunny epidemic. Instead, I found myself asking folks that I knew whether they owned a gun. Specifically, I wanted to learn whether I could borrow their firearm to comfortably sit outside on a lawn chair at night and gleefully pull the trigger to pick off the offending bunnies one by one. I wanted their opinions on the best kind of gun to shoot the bunnies in my yard.

When my wife caught wind of my newfound interest in guns, she instantly shut it down. She told my friends and acquaintances that they were prohibited from lending me a shotgun, rifle, or handgun. They were prohibited from helping me purchase any sort of weapon, and she vociferously explained that no good could come of my owning a gun. Her strong views appeared to derive from her concerns about my lack of experience with guns, rather than any biblical source, coupled with certainty that I would lack competency with any sort of firearm. From her perspective, which she did not hesitate to explain to my male comrades, I was certain to shoot off my foot or worse, accidentally ricochet a bullet right between the eyes of a neighbor. If anyone foolishly aided or abetted me in any way in acquiring a weapon, she would hold them personally responsible for the disastrous outcomes that she predicted. Given her stridency, she scared everyone away from taking me seriously.

My wife's maternal instincts were also at play. She knew that our youngest son, then in elementary school, would have viewed his father as an insanely angry and deranged monster if I harmed a bunny. While my wife was sympathetic to my gardening highs and lows, she thought my lathered-up feelings about the damn wabbits had crossed the line; that it was ridiculous for a grown man and a father to carry on about cute little bunnies running through the yard.

As my frustration with the bunny epidemic simmered, I resorted to an assortment of schemes, such as trying to create a fence of sorts by impaling sticks in the dirt around the peas or beans until they reached a safer height, out of a bunny's reach. If I put in enough sticks around the beds, this seemed to discourage the bunnies, but eventually they became hungry enough to dodge the sticks. My wife's friend told us about coyote blood, which cost a fortune, and we tried sprinkling that around. But each time a good Washington squall washed away the scent, and we had no control over the timing of a heavenly shower. Whatever I tried was unsuccessful.

As the bunny epidemic did not abate, I focused on growing things that the bunnies did not care about, such as red-leafed lettuce, beets, tomatoes, cucumbers, spaghetti squash, and zucchini. I don't know why a rabbit has a voracious appetite for the leaves and stems of peas and string beans, even before they flower, but could care less about the leaves, stems or fruit of tomato plants, but that is the way it is. I learned from trial and error that it is all or nothing in the vegetable beds for the bunnies. Some plants they love and can't get enough of, while others are entirely ignored.

I also bought a kit and with the help of a wonderful friend built an aluminum-framed glass greenhouse that lets me grow bush beans, onions and spinach in pots. The rabbits have not learned how to open the door to the greenhouse. Thus, I reached a détente of sorts with the damn wabbits, although I secretly hoped that the overpopulation of bunnies would produce an epidemic of foxes or raccoons, or alternatively a bunny disease like a rabbit Ebola — or that something, anything, would wipe them out. I fantasized that the bunnies would suddenly disappear as quickly as they had overrun the neighborhood.

My interest in guns revived during a conversation with a neighborhood busybody, a retired realtor who knew what all the houses sold for nearby, who bought them, and why the prior owner moved. Supportive of my gardening, he was also aware of my ongoing frustration with the rabbits. I joked about how my wife vetoed my idea about shooting the rabbits. I explained how I modified what I planted, and how the greenhouse had greatly mitigated the problem. He laughed and said, "Well, given everything you've told me, I should probably stop feeding them."

"What do you mean, feeding them?" I retorted. He told

me that he was feeding them salad and vegetable scraps on his back porch. "Well," I said, "instead of buying a gun to shoot the bunnies, I should buy a gun to shoot you." Although we both laughed, I think we both wondered whether I meant it.

The great thinkers, religious and secular, claim that our passions are sublimated by the human being's ability to reason — and to control where our mind goes to loiter. In a moment of calm, I thought of a solution that didn't involve the greenhouse. I built rectangular frames out of 1" by 2" pieces of wood, cut to fit right on my raised beds. Around the frames I stapled bird netting. The frames are easy to hoist on and off for planting and weeding. Thus, I created a lightweight removable fencing that protects the garden beds from the damn wabbits.

My bunny problem is solved and I am now tolerant of the furry creatures. The damn wabbit calamities seem like they happened decades ago. I am again as I was, not thinking too much about rabbits, and enjoying what grows.

Bay Leaves and Parsley
(Smells)

*Behold, I have given you every herb yielding seed
which is upon the face of all the earth…*
~ Genesis 1:29

I am so proud of our little bay leaf tree. A co-worker of my wife brought cuttings to work and my wife grabbed one. We put it in a pot and it grew in a protected place on the patio for years, until the leaves looked a little sad. It had become root-bound, yearning for liberation from its pot. We found a spot with part sun and part shade, protected from the wind next to a fence, and it thrived. I like to put a mixture of compost and peat moss around its base in the spring, pruning it in the fall. The leaves go into a plastic baggie, usually to give away. I like to use the fresh leaves, which are more aromatic than the dried ones.

Parsley is pretty easy to grow from seed. Parsley evokes the freshness of spring, perhaps because it will usually survive the winter. I grow both the curly kind and Italian parsley, with flat, bigger leaves. I suppose the curly kind is favored as a garnish while the Italian kind is used for cooking. But they both taste great and are interchangeable.

I love cilantro in homemade salsa, or in any Mexican inspired cuisine, and also in Asian style stir fry. Like parsley, cilantro is also easy to grow, a very hardy herb. If you plant it in a garden bed instead of a pot, don't be surprised if volunteers sprout up the next year. When I buy cilantro at the grocery store, I often end up with a gooey, black clump forgotten in the refrigerator before it gets tossed. When I grow cilantro in the home garden, I snip off exactly the harvest that I want, always perfectly fresh and flavorful. The rest keeps growing, so I am never without for the entire summer.

Basil is an annual that is also easy to start from seed. If you cut it regularly, you can keep it going all summer. It likes a nice hot place, so I plant it in the greenhouse. Basil goes great with tomatoes, fish, and cheese dishes. The hardest part is deciding which kind to grow. Sweet basil, with big leaves, or bush basil, with little leaves like a ground cover, are commonly used in Italian cuisine and a variety of soups. Thai basil, perfect for stir-fry, has an anise-clove flavor, and it has purple stems and large green leaves. Lemon and lime basils go great with fish or chicken dishes, or served as a flavorful garnish in a summer cocktail or glass of iced tea.

Mint grows easily in a pot, all the better because otherwise it will spread aggressively and invasively. There are many different kinds of mint to cook with. I like to make tea with fresh peppermint. If you grow mint in a pot, it will become root bound in a single season, but it's such a hardy plant that you can take it out from the pot, slice it into quarters, and it will grow abundantly in four new pots.

If you want to make pickles, you'd better grow garlic and dill. Garlic cloves go in the ground about two inches deep and three inches apart. New bulbs are ready to dig up in about nine months. The garlic plants look similar to leeks, scallions, and shallots, as they are all related to the onion plant. Dill is another annual, but volunteers often pop up the next year like cilantro. A single dill plant likes a lot of sun and can grow several feet tall with skinny, hollow stems and feathery leaves that make flowers like little umbrellas. Sandy soil is best. Dill goes great with salmon, in salad dressings, on soup, and on potatoes.

A kosher dill pickle uses a generous amount of garlic, dill, and salt brine. With one 32-ounce glass jar with a lid, packed full of pickling sized cucumbers, three cloves of garlic, several fresh sprigs of dill, water at room temperature, and two tablespoons of kosher salt, you can make your own dill pickles. Shake the jar with the salt and water, pretending you are a professional bartender, to dissolve the salt. Add everything else. You might also add some other herbs like whole cloves, bay leaves, and an allspice berry. Powdered or ground herbs should be avoided as they will cloud up your brine and turn to sludge on the bottom of the jar. Shake again. Leave the jar out on the countertop for a full day, then alone in the refrigerator for three days. Some people like the crunch and others like the zingy taste, but pickle aficionados will agree there is nothing quite like a classic dill pickle.

Jewish sages tell us that taste and smell are the most refined of all the senses. When we tap into taste and smell, we bypass our intellect and drill directly into deep emotions. That's why eating something mom used to make evokes such comfort. When we sample fresh herbs directly from our own gardens we viscerally and intuitively connect to the natural world and its beneficence. The smell and taste of fragrant herbs comforts our very soul. Herbal life is infused with the Divine Presence.

Reap What You Sow
(Setting an Example)

For all the days of the earth, sowing-time and reaping-time, cold and heat, summer and winter, day and night, shall not cease.

~ Genesis 8:22

One year, the gardeners I knew couldn't stop talking about their tomatoes. No one had ever seen such a prolific crop. In my two raised beds where I grew tomatoes, the plants overgrew their cages and their branches intertwined with each other. I traditionally planted a variety called Stupice due to its smaller size and quick maturity, desirable qualities for a tomato plant in the rainy and cloudy Pacific Northwest. That epic year, my wife canned tomato sauce for the first and only time. When I picked the ripe tomatoes that summer I felt like I was diving into a jungle. I had never seen

the plants so thick. One time, bent over and reaching in to feel for the ripe tomatoes in the overgrown foliage, my prescription glasses fell into the tomato plants and it took over half an hour of clawing around to find them.

Other years will result in great or sparse harvests of different vegetables. One year results in prolific lettuces, another delivers an entire wheelbarrow overflowing with spaghetti squash. Another year the Brussel sprouts are bedeviled by bugs, or an unusually early hot spell causes the spinach to bolt. One never knows exactly how things are going to turn out, despite all the Farmers Almanacs and sophisticated weather forecasts. Thus, the idea that one reaps what one sows, while a good aspirational idea, does not really apply to the garden. One may consistently prepare the garden with great care in a timely manner, but the results may exceed or disappoint expectations.

There are also times when you have to leave town, abandoning the garden during prime growing season. Whoever sets the dates for weddings, funerals, vacations, college graduations, seminars, or business obligations is unlikely to think about the poor gardener involved. You must turn to others to step in and help out, lest the garden dry out and the fruits of your labors rot on the vine.

The next-door neighbor, the kid down the street, a college student home for the summer living just minutes away, or a fellow gardener are all likely suspects to call upon. Unfortunately, your most reliable candidates may also have plans that take them here and there. Thus, you may have to settle on someone whose work is unreliable or subpar, or simply does not have a green thumb. Upon your return, things just don't look the same. Upon examination, some of the plants look horribly abused, especially in the greenhouse where the watering was probably irregular, with days of drought followed by panicky mini-floods.

It is important to keep in mind during these moments that plants are not people. A dead or diseased bush bean does not merit a funeral. An overwatered eggplant does not merit an ambulance ride to a vegetable intensive care facility. You are not facing ruination. Most of what remains in the garden will recover nicely from whatever stresses were suffered with a little tender loving care. The hardier plants, especially the root vegetables like carrots, onions, leeks, and beets, will hardly suffer at all.

The best substitute gardener I ever had was my older son. My younger son was starting college on the east coast in New Haven, Connecticut. Accordingly, my wife and I accompanied him on the plane ride, packing our suitcases to the brim with as much of his stuff as we could cram in to get him through his freshman year of college. The plan was to spend a couple of days schlepping around with the rental car to get whatever else he might need in his dorm room, then travel around New England while he settled in at college, returning at the end of the trip to check back in and say a fond farewell.

My older son and his girlfriend, who lived only an hour away, kindly moved into our house for the purpose of taking care of the garden. The garden thrived under my son's care. Over the course of our journey, he texted pictures of a nicely mowed lawn and a bumper crop of cucumbers. This was heartwarming, as neither son was much interested in gardening when they lived at home. For some reason, they seemed to disappear whenever their mother and I planned to devote a day to weeding. In fact, the most I could usually get out of them was a half day here or there of weed whacking for pay, as weed pulling was clearly beneath their dignity. They liked that their parents had a garden; they even put in a word for certain vegetables. My youngest always wanted me to plant carrots. Yet, gardening was not included in their personal repertoire of favored activities.

As the older one reached his mid-twenties that changed.

When he came over to the house, he asked for a "tour of the garden." He liked to find me in the garden and join in, particularly shoveling the dirt or planting some seeds. He had a wonderful knack for getting the tiniest of the seeds planted, spaced just right, before I discovered seed tape. A few years later when he married the girlfriend and made the transition from apartment dweller to homeowner, he called to ask some questions about gardening. He and his wife were putting a vegetable garden into their little front yard, and he wanted to know what kind of soil to import to his newly self-constructed raised beds. His first year of gardening produced beautiful tomatoes, carrots and peppers. He also met the curious neighborhood children from across the street who visited when he watered. I have the feeling that once his younger brother is no longer an apartment dweller and gets a place of his own with a yard, he will also find the time to till the earth.

One creates a garden not to be chained to it, but to do something wholesome, to establish a healthy and happy place at home where one is comfortably free from the troubles and difficulties of the outside world. Your children may care more about school and their friends, especially when they see you hunched over the dirt weeding the vegetable beds. When they grow up, however, they will know of a way to seek peace, what it means to taste the best of what nature has to offer, and something about the meaning of home.

While different seasons bring variability to the harvest of each vegetable, the cycle that is intrinsic to the garden provides continuity, regularity, and satisfaction. Let your labor in the garden mirror that cycle. The summer and winter, the light and darkness, the time to reap and to sow, are cycles both in nature and the human lifespan. A true home is made into a garden, a model that your children may emulate.

Horseradish
(Bitterness)

*Don't be sweet, lest you be eaten up;
don't be bitter, lest you be spewed out.*
~ Jewish Proverb

My wife came home from book group one early spring with a plastic baggie containing a green leaf attached to dirty white root. She said, "Anne gave me this to give to you."

"What is it?"

"Horseradish."

I put the little scraggly plant into the ground, wondering if it would live.

It looked like a little weed, so I made a mental note to remember that it was horseradish and not to pull it out.

I was surprised how well it did. Within weeks it not only took hold and looked healthy, but it was growing in size, sprouting more leaves. The bunnies ignored it, another plus. By the end of summer, its leaves were gigantic.

"What is that?" asked my kids and several friends, curious about a large leafy plant that they did not recognize. It just kept growing. New horseradish plants seemed to pop up out of the soil inches next to the original one. The big one was over three feet tall. The leaves were large and lush.

I didn't know what to do with it so I waited for the cold weather to hit. After a week of frosty days in November followed by rain storms, the leaves of the plant got limp and fell over. I casually dug up the plant with a hand spade.

What I found was one big tuber feeding a maze of strong smelling roots, most pretty thin, some thicker, shooting this way and that in all directions with no discernible pattern. They broke easily if I pulled on a single root. The big tuber would not pull up at all, as it had too many shoots anchoring it in the soil. This was shovel work. I grabbed a shovel and collected most of the main tuber and a lot of the little shoots. I stopped when I thought I had enough. I washed the collection with the garden hose to get off what dirt I could, and took the odd-looking harvest inside.

The dirty outsides of the roots peeled off easily with a potato peeler. Soon, the entire kitchen smelled like horseradish.

The smell lingered the rest of the day, even after the horseradish went into a plastic bag in the refrigerator, taking up most of the vegetable drawer. Eventually, my wife decided to evict the horseradish and prepare an inaugural batch for consumption. Using a blender the first year and a Cuisinart in succeeding years, my wife grated the horseradish into a mush, added grated beets and white vinegar, ground it further all together and, voila, concocted the best horseradish ever known to humankind.

This did not occur without suffering. We made the mistake of leaning in and sniffing the horseradish mush before adding the vinegar; our eyes burned and inflamed with tears. Our sinuses felt a burning jolt and our noses began to run. Fearing we had rubbed our eyes even though we hadn't, we tried to wash them at the sink, only making matters worse. As we recovered from our temporary blindness, we blew our noses and finished the recipe. By this point we were afraid to taste it, but somehow summoned the courage. Its spiciness was one level down from fiery. We scooped the purple goop into jars to freeze. The one jar that we kept out proved to be really good when we tried it a few days later — fantastic with meat like flank steak or fish like gefilte fish.

The next spring, before I had planted any seeds anywhere, I had ten horseradish plants where there had been one. The plant spread like a virus. Unless I wanted to convert the entire garden into a horseradish farm, an idea I briefly considered and rejected, I knew I had a problem. I had to dig out the roots without breaking them into little pieces, and just leave one plant. Otherwise, I was facing horseradish Armageddon.

After a couple hours of intensive digging, I proved that man could dominate nature, but only temporarily. As the gardening season wore on, new horseradish plants again popped up within inches of the main plant. I attacked immediately, using the shovel and the hand spade, carefully digging up the new plants and their roots, and making certain that no roots broke off. I dug up each shoot back to the main tuber. When it was time to harvest, I spent the time and energy to get as many of the roots shooting off from the main tuber as I could, knowing that I would not get the entire plant, but that I was at least confining it to the designated horseradish area.

The Jews traditionally eat horseradish during the Passover Seder to remind them of the bitterness of slavery in Egypt. Not to minimize the oppressive horrors of slavery, but I wonder if I am a slave to my one horseradish plant. I constantly keep an eye on it and take action immediately to confine its spread.

I love my wife's horseradish condiment. We make just enough to last the year and to give a few jars away, all from just the tuber and roots of one plant. It is really fun and feels unusual to give friends homemade horseradish. We are gifting something bitter that we have made joyful.

But the horseradish plant, for all the bitter pleasure it provides, reminds us that we are not in charge of nature. One horseradish plant, once seeded, can spread uncontrollably if not monitored and contained. In retrospect, it would have been much easier to grow the roots in a large pot to keep it confined.

As human beings, we will suffer bitterness during various points in our lives. The key is to not let the bitterness grow, either by neglect or feelings of being overwhelmed. If there is a bitterness inside of us, we must manage it by confining it and not letting it grow with abandon. In this way we can diminish bitterness within us, allowing it to complement all that is sweet, enhancing the joy in our lives.

Raspberry Jam

(Division of Labor in Marriage)

A woman of valor, who can find? Her worth is far above rubies. The heart of the husband trusts in her and nothing shall he lack. She renders him good and not evil all the days of her life. She opens her hand to the needy, and extends her hand to the poor.

~ Woman of Valor, Eshet Chayil, Proverbs 21

Raspberries found in the grocery store in square little plastic containers sell for the price of gold. I was always too cheap to buy them, but my wife would splurge when it came to raspberries. Amazingly, with some simple cuttings after a couple of seasons, you can cultivate a bountiful raspberry patch with minimal care. You know that you are living well when you step outside on a summer's morning to pick a handful of perfectly ripe raspberries to highlight your breakfast. They will always taste better than what you buy at the store.

To grow raspberries, prepare some soil in a place that gets a nice bit of sun. My neighbor has a patch in the middle of his lawn. He has a big wooden cross on each end of the patch and a metal wire on the end of each cross running to the ends of the other cross to hold up the vines.

I built my raspberry patch along a boundary line fence. I dug up the grass and turned it over with my shovel once a week, waiting a couple of months to let it decompose. Then I covered it with the thinnest weed block that I could find and pounded some left over 2 x 4s horizontally into the ground to create a boundary parallel to the fence. I made little holes in the weed block to plant the raspberry canes. I mulched on top of the weed block to hold it down, to suppress the weeds and to fertilize the canes.

The raspberries spread each spring and new shoots break through the thin weed block, while the dead grass I turned over stays down and decomposes nicely, a feast for the worms. I weed once in the fall when I cut back the canes, before it gets too cold and wet. I weed once again in the spring before the canes fill in. In spring, when the canes sport new growth, I can see which canes are dead and thin those out. After I weed in spring, I add new mulch.

One spring it rained so much that the berries never ripened right. Raspberries get thirsty, but they don't like to sit in a swamp. They don't need as much water as leafy vegetables. I water when it gets hot in the spring or summer, but not too much. You can tell when the raspberries need water just by looking at their leaves.

The raspberries ripen in waves, with a big initial batch after a little heat spell in June, and then ongoing batches ripen throughout July and August. Some of the new shoots even ripen into September. I put my bowl on a lawn chair that I can drag down the line as I pick with two hands. My neighbor puts a string around his neck from which he hangs a cut open milk carton.

If I find some overripe berries when I am picking down the line, I just drop them onto the ground. A raspberry forms a flower that eventually turns into a little quilt of bumps called drupelets. Each little drupelet encloses a seed. Every time I drop a rotten raspberry on the ground, one of the little seeds may find its way to grow another bramble.

The first year that I brought in a gigantic bowl of raspberries, my wife ran to the store to buy pectin and mason jars to make jam. I remember coming in from the yard later that day to spy the miracle of eight beautiful jars full of dark red jam sitting on the counter with sealed lids.

I witnessed and assisted my wife's canning of raspberries many times. This involves boiling and drying the jars and lids, a great deal of mashing, cooking berries with massive amounts of sugar, all without burning one's fingers, while meticulously following the directions that come in every box of jam lids. While I considered my wife's jam making a yearly miracle, eventually she was away on a trip when the berries were ready. Relying on years of observation, but not without great trepidation and several phone calls requesting sage advice from my wife, I proved that even I could make superior jam.

Usually though, we settle on a division of labor in which I grow and pick the berries, and my wife processes the fruit into jam. Once picked, we only have a few days before the berries mold in the refrigerator. We usually end up with enough jars of jam that everyone gets a present. I have been told that our jam is sufficiently revered that it has been hidden from spouses and children, guarded and hoarded as a delicious secret pleasure. When the year's supply of jam begins to diminish, I whine about how little is left, and question the worthiness of the recipient of the most recent jar. My selfish complaints notwithstanding, we seem always to have at least a portion of a jar left in the refrigerator by the time the berries are ready for picking the next year.

As the raspberry patch has flourished over the years and each year's yield has increased, my wife will inevitably tell me at some point in August that she has had it, and absolutely will not make another batch of jam. I am used to these annual outbursts, and my wife's prerogative in our marriage is to say when enough is enough. This does not mean that the raspberries should rot on the vine. My wife has preserved domestic peace by laying out raspberries on a cookie sheet for a few hours in the freezer and then keeping them frozen in plastic bags; they freeze just fine. During winter's gray monotony, it is a pleasure to pull out some frozen raspberries for a special drink made in the blender.

Maintaining a marriage is like gardening. It requires effort and balance so that husband and wife make equal contributions. An equal contribution does not mean that each partner does exactly what the other does. It is relatively easy to grow a horseradish plant and dig up its roots, but it takes a while to clean, peel, and grind the roots, and then add peeled beets and vinegar, to make a nice horseradish sauce. It is easy to pull out some nice spinach and lettuce for a salad, but it is laborious to clean the leaves.

The division of labor between garden and kitchen usually

just happens; it may evolve without negotiation, and without significant bitterness or resentment because of the goodness that results from a joint effort. The garden lends itself to sharing, and to a deepening of the relationship between couples. Raspberry jam is not male or female itself. It is admired and enjoyed regardless of who grew the berries or who made the jam.

Mr. Mole
(Ethics of Hunting)

A man should consider himself as a worm, and all other small animals his friends in the world, for all them are all created.

~ Baal Shem Tov

One fat little mole can burrow through a yard at night, surfacing often enough to create unsightly mounds of dirt all over, like acne on a lawn. I've tried every product on the shelves of the big-box home and garden stores, including different pellets and poisons, and smoke bombs with catchy names. I have also resorted to the home remedy of the garden hose to try to flush the despicable grub-eaters out of their tunnels, all in vain.

I have given endless pep talks to our cat, Kittyakavich, to "do her job" and "bring daddy Mr. Mole." But our cat is clearly not a "moler" and instead prefers a steady diet of little birds and baby rabbits in the spring and summer, animals that she likes to bring to our patio door so she can show us her prey. We have grown accustomed to hearing their final tweets and beeps on many a warm summer's eve, right outside the screen door. Although Kittyakavich clearly prefers birds and bunnies, she will leave an occasional rat or mouse tail by the door. Kittyakavich is clearly not a picky eater, so I don't know why other people are blessed with cats who are "molers" and we are not.

My neighbor was kind enough to show me his bucket of mole traps, explaining that it was probably just one mole pushing up all the mounds in both of our yards. I promptly went out and bought a couple traps of my own. We made a neighborly agreement that whoever caught a mole was entitled to a dinner out. Before too long, I trapped a mole and we enjoyed a celebratory dinner with our wives. After my initial success trapping a mole, I bought more traps the next year.

Trapping a mole is not quite like catching a fish. When a Coho salmon jerks the fishing line and starts to run, you experience great excitement as the battle begins to bring in a beautiful fish. Taking the fish out of the net, we admire its silvery shiny colors and scales.

The mole is not beautiful. It has a weird little hairless snout, the tiniest beady eyes, and disproportionately outsized webbed claws for digging.

Here is how I set a mole trap. I cut the ground with my shovel straight down in a circle around the mole hill. I am trying to carve out a nice piece of grass sod that I will use to cover the trap. Once I dig my hole, I feel around to find where the tunnels are. Interestingly, the tunnels are never in a straight line across from each other, but rather always at an angle. Sometimes, it is surprisingly difficult to find both tunnels, but keep feeling around the dirt in the sides of your hole. I guarantee that you will find entrances to both sides of the tunnel. Cocking a trap to set it into a hole requires a couple of tongs that allows you to spread out the jaws, essentially two sets of killer scissors that spring shut if the mole triggers it.

When I place the sprung trap into the hole, I angle and align it to allow the mole to enter the trap from either end. I like to place any rocks that I found digging the hole to the sides of the trap to help guide the mole into the trap. I use the sod I dug up, plus nearby leaves or fallen twigs, to cover the hole, then I pack dirt over the top of the trap and the hole, as Mr. Mole likes things nice and dark. I push one stick in the ground to remind me where I placed each mole trap.

Whereas bringing that Coho into the boat is always a happy moment, pulling a trap out with the jaws snapped tight through some portion of the anatomy of Mr. Mole is a traumatizing experience. Typically, I scream. It may take me a few deep breaths to calm down before I extricate the remains of Mr. Mole from the trap. Thereafter, I run like the wind to get my wife, and together we shovel Mr. Mole in a plastic bag that we tie securely and deposit in the garbage can.

Once the trauma of finding dead Mr. Mole almost sliced in two dissipates, the lawn is free of unsightly mole mounds for the rest of the season, or until another mole meanders into the neighborhood. Thus, the garden remains pimple-free only for a time.

I have recently learned that mole traps are illegal in my state. A voter initiative banning body gripping animal traps that exempted mouse traps failed to exempt mole traps. Possibly that was an oversight, but nonetheless it rendered mole traps illegal. Yet they remain available in the stores with common garden supplies and devices. Further, I do not believe the local fish and game constables are likely to be on the lookout for the home mole trapper. No one advocates or lobbies for Mr. Mole and his ilk.

While I have adopted a live-and-let-live attitude in regard to most of God's creepy and crawly creatures in and around my garden, relying on nature to keep the good bugs and bad bugs in balance, my aesthetic values are offended by Mr. Mole's activities. I am not dissuaded from using an illegal trap to kill Mr. Mole even when I am told that the mole is beneficially aerating the soil. Mr. Mole's unsightly mounds offend my eye. Human beings legitimately strive to create beauty. For better or worse, I belong to the human race.

Sometimes I lack compassion and understanding and, to make matters worse, even though I understand that I lack compassion and understanding, I stubbornly maintain my lack. My insight doesn't soften me; I ignore it.

Sometimes I am much more like Kittyakavich, hunting birds and bunnies with impunity, than a human being who should be striving for righteousness. I am overtaken by my own reptilian brain. The difference is the cat is supposed to act like a cat, whereas I rationalize my sins. I question why the Master of the Universe would create such a miserable looking creature to disturb the aesthetics of my lawn and garden. It is difficult for me to visualize Noah shepherding a pair of moles onto the ark. How can I honestly say that I cleave to God when I break the law and place appearances ahead of mercy? How can I love God when I honestly do not love all of what He created? Maybe I can do without the mole traps this year; I don't know. We'll see.

The Green House
(Having a Best Friend)

A faithful friend is a powerful defense;
he that has found such a one has found a treasure.
~ BEN SIRA 6:14

SOMETIMES an ephemeral dream becomes a reality, albeit with a little help from a good friend. This idea may float in and out of your cerebrum for years, never staying put long enough, like a passing shadow, to take hold.

I always wanted a greenhouse, but it seemed like a pipe-dream. There were other priorities for our family and for our humble abode. For a long time I did not get as far as thinking about the practical questions of where the greenhouse might go, who would build it, or how much it would cost. A greenhouse was just a fleeting fantasy.

Just like the miracle of a tiny seed's germination, a human

being has the capacity to plant the kernel of an idea — from an elusive longing — and let it start to grow. To transform the thought into action, the idea has to stick in your consciousness like a gymnast's hard dismount. Eventually I started an investigation on the internet, which soon overloaded me with too much information. There were more greenhouse ideas, advertisements, and recommendations than I ever imagined. There were too many options to choose from, but I decided that a greenhouse finally seemed both possible and practical.

I suggested an outing with my spouse to attend the local home and garden show. Rather than look at pictures or videos on the internet, doubters like myself want to see examples up close. Where I live, these trade shows come every wintertime, usually after the boat show and the RV show.

One cautionary note about attending a trade show: If you are anything like me, you may come home with a $500.00 Vitamix blender sold at a special show price of $399.99, or $20.00 worth of special skin cream made from a unique variety of coconuts that can only be found on the island of Sri Lanka. I confess that I am a sap for the latest chopper, slicer, dicer, and grater which, I am told, is not available anywhere else. The friendly person selling the gadget will heartily explain how easy it is to use all twelve dishwasher-safe pieces that take up hardly any space. I find myself fishing out my wallet to buy one even before the spiel ends.

While home improvement contractors dominated the show, there were also plenty of gardening exhibits featuring compost bins and worm farms, fountains, rocks, patios, statuary, "garden art," sheds, garden furniture, irrigation systems, seeds, hoses, gloves, birdhouses, and finally, at the end of aisle M, an exhibitor with a couple of models of greenhouses. Unfortunately, the first models I saw on display were made of plastic, looked flimsy and cheaply made, though priced to move. Leaving the fairgrounds, toting my impulse purchases, I was disappointed like a teenager after a first date gone wrong.

While pursuing an unrelated errand weeks later, I drove by a sign that said, "The Glass Gardener" and saw out of the corner of my eye greenhouses on the side of the road. Executing a quick U-turn, I found what I wanted: a display of greenhouses of different sizes made of aluminum frames with glass panels. The materials for the frames came from England, while the glass was purchased locally. The frames came in kits with the glass cut for each kit. Costs averaged from a little less than one thousand dollars to a little more than three thousand dollars, with the kit delivered to your home to assemble yourself. For an extra five hundred bucks, they offered to come to your house and put it together for you. The model I chose measured 17 x 8 feet. Building the foundation consisted of leveling the ground, using 4 x 6-inch treated landscape timbers to affix into a rectangle with brackets, upon which the frame would sit, then laboriously filling the inside with a couple yards of pea gravel, leveling that out, and covering it with a thick black landscape fabric. This allowed water to easily drain through the landscape fabric into the gravel.

Like a fool I chose the do-it-yourself option, saving $500. Laying out everything on the driveway, I was aghast at the number of pieces. I also discovered, to my horror, that in my enthusiasm and anxious zeal to get started, I'd torn open the cardboard boxes and took out the aluminum pieces without noticing that the printing on the boxes provided the only labeling for the pieces. The written directions consisted of 32 pages of numbers and schematics that looked like Egyptian hieroglyphics. The cardboard boxes now sat in a big heap. Feeling panicked, I started trying to group and lay out the pieces as they might go together.

I was in the midst of this crisis, feeling forlorn, when my friend David drove up. David grew up on a farm in Nebraska and thought it would be fun to help build the greenhouse. A true friend lends a hand; he is someone you can lean on, someone who brings calm when your psychic balance is on TILT and you are feeling the weight of being alone. David was such a friend.

Completely ignoring the frustration in which I was enveloped, David announced: "I think it goes like this. We don't need those directions." We set to work with the screws, washers and bolts. David led the charge for the next several hours as the frame took shape, only finally consulting the directions for the doors and the windows.

The windows on the roof had a wax mechanism to allow for automatic opening and closing depending on the temperature. This intrigued David immensely, as if learning about the wax window openers had justified all of his free labor. The bottom line was that my greenhouse went up efficiently thanks to my friend, someone I trusted who knew what he was doing, even if he had never constructed a greenhouse before. He even brought an old table from his garage that he thought would fit well in the greenhouse as a work bench.

The glass panels were very well labeled and I spent another full day, this time by myself, snapping them into place with metal brackets, a repetitive exercise that punished my thumbs until they were raw. Not without effort and expenditure, I could now stand back and admire the idea of a greenhouse having become a reality.

The location of the greenhouse luckily provided for excellent morning sun and was slightly shaded by the garage in the late afternoon. But there was too much mid-afternoon sun. I hung a mesh shade screen from the ceiling of the greenhouse to help buffer it. For containers I bought 2 x 4-foot ceramic chimney flues that kept the soil warm. I mixed compost, peat moss, and vermiculite in equal thirds to fill the containers. I bought varieties of tomato and cucumber seeds specifically recommended to grow in greenhouses.

Cucumbers pop up before tomatoes in the greenhouse. Seedless cucumbers do not require pollination and can establish strong roots in the dirt mixture in the chimney flues on the sunniest side of the greenhouse. The trick is to train the cucumber plant up a trellis by removing lateral branches and taking off the bottom leaves. If the plant gets too long for the trellis, it will hang over for a couple of feet. At that point it may make sense to pinch off the plant rather than let the greenhouse become a cucumber jungle.

Tomatoes can likewise train to a single stem to grow with support from a trellis. For varieties that are better left untrained, like cherry tomatoes, a tomato cage fits well into the chimney flues. The cage is needed to support the plant. I like to tear off pieces of biodegradable garden tape that adheres to itself to tie unruly stems to the cages.

You have to flick or lightly shake the buds and flowers of tomato plants to make sure fruit forms. When the outside garden beds finally warm enough to plant starts, the greenhouse gardener may already be harvesting the first cucumbers of the season.

The greenhouse is also a great place to start pots by seed for cucumbers, tomatoes, spaghetti squash, and zucchini that can be transplanted outside when the weather warms up. Also, annual ornamentals for the garden including sunflowers, marigolds, zinnia, phlox, cosmos, and dianthus, to name a few, are also fun to start by seed in the greenhouse. By growing your own, you can transfer ornamentals to the flower beds at the optimum time, before the containers become root bound. Some of these flowers will keep going all summer with a lot of color, even into September, October, and perhaps November. My cosmos flowers are taller than I am by late August and typically last into November. If you clip the spent flowers, new flowers will continue to blossom.

The joy of gardening is extended with the greenhouse because you can start earlier and end later in the year. The greenhouse is its own warm little world, protected from the rabbits and the crows. It is calm when the wind is blowing and dry when the rain is falling. Greenhouse plants will survive a late spring snow or an early fall frost. Weeds are rare.

Still, as I sing the praises of owning my own greenhouse, I acknowledge how fortunate I was to have my friend David to put it together. As Ecclesiastes 4: 9-10 says, "Two are better than one, because they have a good return for their work. For if they fall, the one will lift up his fellow; but woe to him that is alone when he falls, for he has no one to help him up."

David always acts surprised when I bring him one of the first cucumbers of the season from the greenhouse. When he visits, he always smiles when he pokes his head inside. He likes to see what I've got going on in there.

Planting Trees
(Caring for the Natural World)

*Rabbi Yochanan ben Zakkai used to say,
"If you have a sapling in your hand and you are told
that the Messiah has come, first plant the sapling
and then go and meet the Messiah."*
~ Avot de Rabbi Natan 31b

THE spiritual gardener is invariably drawn to places where trees are allowed to grow. Leave your car and step into a forest. Your immediate payoff is the serenity and peace that you feel when surrounded by natural beauty. You pass the gate or trailhead and all is good, life is fulfilling, as it should be. You have no complaints or grudges to harbor against your fellow human beings. Consciously or not, you feel joy, and a unity with the Creator of the Universe. Viscerally, soulfully, and intuitively you want to praise God for creating such wondrous beneficence.

Parks, gardens and forests provide entirely natural or specifically designed spaces with one common thread. They all have trees. Trees live longer than humans; some trees, like the redwoods of northern California, may live several thousand years. Trees have roots, trunks, and branches that all grow silently, often unnoticed by us, due to how slowly they change over long lifespans. Trees survive catastrophic storms better than most human edifices. Their astounding diversity may include over 100,000 species. The beneficent gardener venerates trees with spiritual and emotional wonderment.

I have three cedar trees in my yard, and a boundary line with one neighbor of large fir trees. I have two beautiful ornamental trees, one false chestnut and one catalpa, which produce beautiful spring flowers. Finally, I have several Japanese maples. All of these trees add beautiful color and contrast to the garden. Trees soundscape the garden, adding pleasant bird notes and reducing annoying urban sounds.

Occasionally, when weeding a flower bed, I come across a naturally growing sapling of a tree. I can either leave it there, or pick it out like a weed, or dig it up carefully and transfer it to a pot. Given my penchant for vegetable gardening and a desire to keep the beds in full sun, I usually choose to transfer any newfound tree sapling to a pot. This buys a couple of years' time before the plant will become root bound, and then I can either plant the tree somewhere in the yard or give it away. I have never seen anyone disappointed by the gift of a tree.

If you have a beautiful ornamental tree or any number of flowering bushes like rhododendrons, a simple trick is to take a cutting in spring or summer. Find a stem with new growth of about four or five inches with healthy leaves and cut it off. Gently shave off an inch or two of just a very thin layer of the bark at the bottom of the cutting, dip the shaved portion into root hormone that you can buy at any nursery, and plant the cutting in a pot. Keep it outside, but in a protected area. More likely than not, the cutting will take root and survive the next winter. It is always fun to grow a new bush or tree from a cutting.

I confess that I am a tree hugger. I derive a lot of pleasure from trees. I don't know when my affinity with trees began; the first memory I have of anyone talking about trees occurred in Sunday school. I have several certificates from the Jewish National Fund dating back to 1961 with my name on them. Each says, **"TREE PLANTED IN ISRAEL by Andy Becker."** In 1961 I was seven years old. The Sunday school teacher gave us a cardboard cut-out with holes to put in dimes. The dimes were the leaves in the cardboard picture of a tree. When the leaves were filled up with dimes, you brought it back and turned it in. Each set of dimes meant another tree was planted in Israel.

The certificates had two rows of Cypress trees on the sides and barren hills in the background as decoration. At age seven, this exercise created vague questions in my mind. I wondered: Was a tree really planted? How big was it? Where was it planted? And how would anyone know it was "my" tree? I was a born skeptic.

I don't remember my Sunday school teacher explaining the ecological benefits of trees in regard to soil erosion, wildlife habitat, flood prevention, or beautification. Atmospheric climate change was not on anyone's radar. What I remember being told was that Israel had barren lands that desperately needed trees. The point was that we were doing something good for Eretz Yisrael, the Land of Israel.

Putting dimes into pieces of cardboard, notwithstanding the encouragement to do so and the later receipt of a fancy paper certificate, did not create a bond between me, then aged single digits, and the land of Israel. Instead, it created an image of Israel as a hot and barren place without many trees. Israel seemed like a rather unattractive place. Also, I did not feel joy putting dimes into the cardboard, as a significant fraction of my life savings disappeared each time I had enough dimes to hand in.

My mistaken childhood impressions were put to rest when I traveled to Eretz Yisrael as an adult. I learned that although Israel had hot, barren, desert areas, trees were abundant in lush green orchards and evergreen forests; willows and poplars grew along rivers meandering through parched land. I visited an ancient green oasis with palm trees fed by springs and waterfalls, known for thousands of years to be hidden in a canyon of the desert.

Whether visiting the Holy Land or wherever your footsteps take you, please consider the trees around you. Doesn't God ask us to look after and cultivate the beautiful trees in the garden that God created? After all, Adam's first mission was to tend the Garden of Eden. And God first spoke to Moses in a burning bush, underscoring that what grows in nature is infused with the Divine.

Physically planting a tree is a joyful, sensual and often sentimental experience. You pick what tree to plant and where to plant it, sizing up the landscape, and thinking aesthetically. You create a space for the young tree and then give it a protective ring. The roots go into the hole that you dug and watered. Your hands carefully dislodge the tree from its pot, then you place the tree in the hole and cover the dirt around the sapling's roots. You are participating in nature's design, putting something into the ground that will grow to be beautiful and majestic. The tree that you plant is likely to be around longer than you. Perhaps you have planted this particular tree in honor of your newborn, your marriage, moving into your new house, or some other special occasion. Maybe you planted it just for the heck of it. As the tree that you planted grows and changes with the seasons you will notice it from time to time, more than others. As the years pass, and the tree survives many a bitter storm, you may feel a very particular affinity for that tree.

I wish we could take every elementary school child on a field trip to plant a sapling, help replenish a forest or fruit orchard, beautify a park, or add to our urban landscape. Let's teach that soil is not something to just walk on or pave over, to drive on, but the very ground of our being; our source of nourishment.

We can learn a lot from trees, especially their firmly anchored roots and perseverance during stormy times. The learned sages from the Talmud (Avot 3:22) tell us that if you have many branches and few roots, a wind can turn your tree upside down. If you have few branches and many roots, even if all winds of the world were to blow, you will not be budged from your place. Let's stay anchored, as human beings, to our beautiful universe, and feel our own roots in the natural world every day, but especially every time we plant a cutting of an ornamental bush, and every time we plant a tree.

The Old Catalpa
(Old Age)

If not for the trees, human life could not exist.
~ Midrash Sifre (Deuteronomy) 20:19

Trees and plants have a language of their own.
~ Baal Shem Tov

THE Old Catalpa tree was a haven for the birds each spring. As the Catalpa's leaves grew again, songbirds established their nests, hidden by the Catalpa's floppy green leaves. The nestlings became all but invisible, although their chirping and their parents' frequent excursions to bring food to the nests confirmed their presence. April often brought a couple of teaser days, when the clouds parted and the temperature warmed enough to sit outside and soak in the sun's warmth while listening to the constant cries for food from the baby birds.

    The old Catalpa was also a jungle gym for children, mostly boys around age nine or ten, who could not resist climbing the trunk, starting where it had a big bump to ascend to the main branches. Eventually, the tree started growing some weeds up there, where the leaves pooled and a neighborhood raccoon left some scat. The Catalpa also had lots of holes higher up where the woodpeckers hollowed out its branches. But the old tree continued to grow majestically year after year. The tree's jasmine scented flowers always bloomed late and when a late July wind storm blew in, the white flowers fell, en masse, covering the grass below like a summer's snow. Sitting between the house and the afternoon sun, the Catalpa was the home's air conditioner, providing needed shade during the hottest afternoons of August and September. In November and December, the Catalpa made a huge mess when all the leaves came down, and it was a hassle to rake up all the leaves. But that forced us outside to get some exercise when we would otherwise be homebound on chilly winter days.

    When a big Catalpa branch came down with an earth-shaking boom, I was on the other side of the house mowing the lawn with the John Deere. I had just mowed the Catalpa side of the yard minutes before. I heard a very loud crash and had no idea what it was. As I raced around the house, I could see that the Catalpa's largest branch had sheared off the main part of the tree, bringing down other branches with it. Curiously, the most vulnerable looking spots where the woodpeckers had carved out holes were still intact. Yet, it was clear that the tree was a hazard, and we were lucky it had not fallen on anyone. We had not realized how dangerous it was, but we loved that tree so much that we had turned a blind eye to how it had rotted even as it continued to grow. We were so used to that tree that we paid a pretty penny to the local nursery to order us a young one that we planted as close as we could to where the old Catalpa had stood.

The old Catalpa had something for everyone: a home for the birds, a playground for the children, and cooling shade for the house. The yard looked empty without it, even after we planted the new little Catalpa. We knew that it would take years for the new to rival the old.

Our culture celebrates youthful vitality, viewing old age as a liability. It is true that physically we will weaken, decay and break, just like an old tree. But our old Catalpa was at its most majestic and beneficent in its old age. The strength of its branches had weakened and its days were numbered, but the soul of that tree, and what it provided in its environment, grew richer and more valuable each year, until it finally crashed.

The sages of the Talmud tell the story of an old man who was planting a tree. A young man passed by and asked him what he was planting. The old man told the young one that he was planting a carob tree. The youth asked critically, "Don't you know that it takes 70 years for a carob tree to bear fruit?"

"That's okay," said the old man. "Just as others planted for me, I plant for future generations."

As we age, we need not retire from the garden or any other meaningful pursuit. Our souls do not retire. It may hurt our arthritic necks a little more each year to pull the weeds, but we know what, where, and when to plant; we know how to grow our garden better and better each year; and we have more time to engage in activities that are priceless. When we beautify a yard, we not only please the eye, we create a playground, provide an environment for living creatures, and turn the barren into the cultivated. Just as the Catalpa's leaves seek the sun, our souls yearn for relevance, even when resting under the shade of a favorite tree.

Borscht
(Diversity)

Borscht is the center of everything.
~ Ukrainian Proverb

The old adage that "variety is the spice of life" may be rooted in the amazing diversity of plants. Even among traditional early spring garden vegetables like beets, radishes, and spinach, there seems to be an infinite variety. Beets and radishes come in almost all the colors of the rainbow, from purple to red to pink to white, and grow in different shapes, from balls to cylinders. Yet for all the different colors and shapes, there is much less variation in taste. Beets have a slightly sweet, earthy taste while radishes taste crisp and a little hot. Spinach, always green, with variations in shape and texture, has an earthy and mineral taste.

Surprisingly, many people will tell you that they don't like beets, radishes or spinach. The folks who generally turn up their noses to fresh vegetables are often addicted to processed foods. The enthusiastic gardener is a warrior against foods that come in boxes and wrappers, chemical concoctions that have helped create the epidemic of obesity and related diseases like high blood pressure and diabetes.

The incredible diversity of root and leafy vegetables makes me think of Borscht, an ancient soup that has more variations than ways to cook cod in Portugal. The borscht that I like best is dark red, almost purple, with a base of vegetable stock dominated by beets and finished off with a dollop of sour cream. The white sour cream highlights the color of the beets until mixed into the soup to turn the rich red into a soft pink, also delivering a contrasting sour taste to the sweetness of the beets. You can eat borscht hot, to warm from a wintry chill, or cold, to cool off from the summer heat.

I want to let you in on a secret. Even a small garden creates all you need to make a phenomenal vegetable stock. Just four cups of vegetables makes two quarts of vegetable stock. Onions, carrots, celery, leeks, lettuce, potatoes, tomatoes, parsnip, green beans, chard, squash, peppers, you name it, all go into the pot. If you can add clean and healthy roots, leaves, stalks, and peelings — all the stuff you might otherwise compost or throw away — so much the better. Chop everything pretty small to infuse more flavors, start with cold water, and let it simmer slowly for half an hour after coming to a boil.

Once you have vegetable stock you are ready to make borscht. Simply cut up beets, onions, carrots, and cabbage into shreds and matchsticks, sauté, add a little lemon juice, and then add the stock, salt, and pepper. You may improvise with anything else in the garden that's ready: potatoes, peppers, beans, or herbs. You decide whether to emulsify some, none, or all of the vegetables. One borscht is often very different than another, but borscht is borscht.

The alchemy of a garden manifests in a homemade bowl of borscht. Divine sparks in each scrap of each vegetable have dissolved together, liberating and blending a diversity of flavors. A fine bowl of borscht is indeed worthy of a blessing before the meal.

The great sages ordained that one should not benefit from this world without first reciting a blessing. A simple blessing in Hebrew recited before eating vegetables is, "Baruch atah A-donay, Elo-heinu Melech Ha'Olam, borei pri ha-adamah." "Blessed are You, Lord our God, King of the Universe, who creates the fruit of the earth." Thus we transform a meal, otherwise mundane, into a holy act.

Buen provecho, buon appetite, chi la te shin ye, vel become, esgezunterheyt! Please enjoy your borscht. It will taste even better tomorrow.

Abundant Garden, Abundant Peace
(Benefits of Gardening)

The best remedy for those who are afraid, lonely, or unhappy is to go outside, somewhere where they can be quite alone with the heavens, nature and God. Because only then does one feel that all is as it should be and that God wishes to see people happy, amidst the simple beauty of nature. As long as this exists, and it certainly always will, I know that then there will always be comfort for every sorrow… And I firmly believe that nature brings solace in all troubles.

~ Diary of Anne Frank

Although gardening is work, the rewards are numerous. A raised bed of dirt in March becomes a bonanza of spinach, radishes, lettuce, and broccoli by May. The vegetables please the eye with their contrasting colors and shapes. Growing one's own organic food that tastes great, picked timely, right at home, leads to a happy excitement.

As one's gardening skills improve from trial and error, year to year, the produce improves in size and quality. As the garden flourishes, one's spirits lift. The garden has a calming quality, cooling us naturally from over-stimulated lives. On a Sunday morning, as the birds chirp away, much weeding, seeding, harvesting and watering can be accomplished in a short period of time. Why addict oneself to images on a rectangular electronic screen when one can smell the soil and breathe in the weather? Why not ground oneself in the reality of the earth's abundance?

"Home Sweet Home" means a place of serenity and relaxation where one feels most comfortable. A home with a garden is a happier, healthier, and friendlier home. The home garden is the antithesis of conflict and violence found elsewhere; it is a reservoir of peace. A home garden projects an inner comfort where one dwells, an actual warmth that can be found within the gardener. The lusher the garden, the more respectful all those who pass by or enter.

I do not know anyone who experienced depression picking the first strawberry of the year. I encourage everyone to take advantage of their yards and start planting. We can fill the countryside, the suburbs, and the inner cities with garden plots. Something will usually grow somewhere. Look at the Douro Valley in Portugal, a World Heritage Site for wine vineyards, where the hillsides are steep, water is scarce, and the ground is terribly rocky. Grapes have been grown there for generations and turned into exceptional wines.

If we planted much of our vacant land, neighbors would encounter each other outside. They would inevitably meet and talk to one another. Co-workers would bring their excess zucchinis, tomatoes, and cucumbers to the job site or office for everyone to share.

Just by gardening, we could straighten out some of the distortions in the world. If humankind wants to stop its descent into unending conflict, decadence and immorality, the garden path can help us reverse course and create a harvest of beauty, abundance, and health.

During the time you are busy gardening, you can forget your resentments and complaints and become absorbed in the task at hand. Like accountants itemizing expenditures, we spend so much time adding up our hurts and wrongs. When we let go of our long list of grievances, we can restore the soul. Our grievances are painful, and pain fills us with loneliness. In the garden, shepherding natural growth for our own nutrition helps us forget the sad songs that tend to play over and over again in our brains.

With a pervasive spread of gardening in our country, I

predict that the levels of violence, crime, and stress would decrease. I would like to see our food banks overflow. No one should go hungry. We can even put gardens in our schools, jails, and mental institutions. If I were running for President, my slogan would be, "Fresh carrots and onions for everyone!"

It is not hard to start a garden. I began with four raised beds. I used scrap 2"x 8"s, built into rectangles, 12 feet x 4 feet. I placed them on the flattest and sunniest part of the yard over dirt that I had turned over. I ordered a load of topsoil and had them dump it as close to the frames as possible. With a half day of wheel barrow work, the pile of dirt was moved to the beds, and the beds were ready for planting.

I learned year by year. Peas need something to climb up; crows will try to eat your corn before you can pick it; not all the seeds you plant will sprout. And you'll never have enough room for everything you want to plant.

The first expansion consisted of seventy-five feet of raspberries along a fence where I had two raspberry plants that seemed to grow well. The next expansion consisted of four more raised beds. When a boundary line hedge died due to a cruel winter, I pulled out the dead hedge and noticed that I had a line of soft rich soil. I planted another 75 feet of vegetables the next summer.

Although there is additional room in my yard for more beds, I have all the garden I can handle for now. Of the eight raised beds, our single beds are dedicated individually to asparagus, strawberries, cucumbers, and tomatoes, leaving four raised beds where I plant red lettuce, baby romaine lettuce, spinach, radishes of different varieties, green onions, peas, beets, leeks, Brussel sprouts, carrots and broccoli. These four beds involve replanting more spinach, carrots, onions, and lettuce, depending when I pull out the first batches.

The long bed bordering my other fence is perfect for one crazy horseradish plant, four blueberry bushes, spaghetti squash, and cucumbers. I try to separate the squash and cucumbers with several feet of additional beets and onions. Otherwise, the spaghetti squash, which is naturally yellow to light tan in color, cross-pollinates with the cucumbers and ends up green.

I recommend that you start your new garden with some seeds or starts that grow easily and abundantly. In the Pacific Northwest, zucchini is as reliable as the rain. I like the Italian kind best. Zucchini likes a lot of sun. It has a large flat seed that you can start indoors, as the seed needs warmth to germinate. Once the temperature outside warms up, watch out, as the zucchinis take off. You can pick them any size you want, from four inches to a foot, or let them grow as big as a lopsided baseball bat. I guarantee that if you plant a couple of zucchinis once the soil warms up, by August and September you will have so many that you will be giving them away. We know that generosity is a virtue. Giving away what you grew is just as great a gift to the giver as to the receiver. The zucchini that you give away you will not miss.

I find that most years we give away zucchinis, tomatoes, cucumbers, spaghetti squash, radishes, and lettuce. Additionally, as special and coveted presents, we give away raspberry jam, strawberry jam, and our own horseradish sauce made with vinegar and beets.

How often do we have more than we need in life? We like to acquire possessions, and we overflow with wants and desires. We usually hang on to more possessions, wants and desires than we need. However, with a simple garden plot, we are unlikely to hoard that which we cannot consume. It is natural for those who garden to practice generosity with family, friends, co-workers, and neighbors. Let as many of us as possible make our homes into gardens. A land full of beneficent gardens can transform a trembling world into a world of joy. Let us beat our swords into plowshares, our spears into pruning hooks. And let us all say together, **AMEN!**

About the Author

Andy Becker is a writer, gardener, and lifetime learner, who lives in Western Washington among the cedar trees with his wife Donna and their two dogs, Nova and Splash. Andy was a successful small-town lawyer who found respite from the vicissitudes of fighting for the little guy against insurance companies by gardening, hiking, and camping with his family, and by expanding his spirituality through Judaism. During his early years of gardening, he was often frustrated, beset by rocky soil, hills, and too many slugs and deer. Despite these challenges, Andy has never failed to grow vegetables every spring and summer. His current garden includes a greenhouse, eight raised beds, a thirty-yard vegetable bed, and a forty-yard stretch of raspberry vines.

His first published book, *The Spiritual Gardener: Insights from the Jewish Tradition to Help Your Garden Grow,* is an illustrated gift book coupling spiritual themes with gardening tasks to inspire gardening and well-being. *The Spiritual Gardener* won the New York City Big Book Award in the Home and Garden category.

Andy's second book, *Cracking an Egg,* is a humorous and heartfelt look at early childhood experiences growing up in the 1960s.

Andy's third book and debut novel, *The Kissing Rabbi: Lust, Betrayal, and a Community Turned Inside Out,* is the first #MeToo novel where the antagonist is a young ultra-orthodox rabbi. After building a vibrant community from scratch, the rabbi botches his misguided attempts at the seduction of several congregants and creates a scandal that rocks the community. *The Kissing Rabbi* won a First Place Chanticleer Mark Twain Award for humor and satire.

Andy's most recent book, *The Spiritual Forest: Timeless Jewish Wisdom for a Healthier Planet and a Richer Spiritual Life,* is his second book in his Spiritual Garden series. *The Spiritual Forest* encourages us to cultivate our trees and forests as a vital source of life so we can connect to the earth and our spirituality in a deeply transformational way.

If you read and like any of Andy's books, please post a favorable review online. For more information about Andy's books, see **www.andybecker.life**. Write directly to Andy at **andybecker.life@gmail.com**

Made in United States
Troutdale, OR
02/27/2024

17986820R00075